SELLING IT SOFTLY

*Create your own story
of direct sales success*

SUE RUSCH

Published by:

GRAND
OAKS
PRESS

Grand Oaks Press
7455 France Avenue South #507
Minneapolis, MN 55435

ISBN: 978-1-4675-3307-2

Printed in the United States of America.
First Printing: June 2010
Second Printing: July 2012

Dedicated to the memory of my mother,

Bertha Eleanor Rohrbach,

and to possibilities.

For ease of reading, direct sellers and their customers are referred to in the female gender throughout this book. Direct selling success, of course, is available to men and women. Use of the female gender is not intended to exclude the increasing male population involved in the business of direct selling.

Throughout the book, names have been changed to preserve anonymity.

CONTENTS

PREFACE

It took me a while to take selling seriously. Kind of odd for someone writing a sales training book.

When I was new to the business of selling 30 years ago, a friend told me, *Sue, once you learn to sell, you can do anything!* At the time, I didn't get it. To me, selling was just a job, a way of making a living. I didn't expect the experience of selling to have a profound impact on every dimension of my life.

Discovering that selling is foundational to every element of life and business success, I devoured whatever training I could get my hands on. Books about selling introduced me to new words, phrases, and techniques to enhance my sales presentation. I noticed that many traditional selling techniques were well-suited for a business or retail selling environment, but not always applicable to the business I was in: direct selling.

I didn't sell in boardrooms or retail stores. I sold in living rooms. Sisters connected with sisters, and friends connected with friends, as I sold in their homes. In my workplace, hostesses hugged their friends at the door, and sometimes even gave me a warm hug as I left their homes at the end of the night. Where I worked, mothers and grandmothers chatted tenderly with their grown daughters. I was a direct seller, and my way of selling felt somehow different. It felt *softer*.

I was one of the 15.8 million* people who call *direct sales* their way of doing business. I would spend most of my career learning to sell effectively and defining my approach for other sales professionals. This book is the result.

* Source: www.directselling411.com

So let's take a hard look at *Selling It Softly*. Since the 2010 release of this book, readers have told me it has inspired them to rethink what it means to sell. They've told me that where the fear of being perceived as "pushy" once interfered with their ability to succeed, the underlying principles of selling with softness have now changed the course of their businesses. They tell me they feel more confident and proud to be a sales professional. My heart has been warmed by their stories of how *Selling It Softly* has strengthened their resolve to keep moving forward, even when it feels hard.

WHAT IS DIRECT SELLING?

The Direct Selling Association defines direct selling:

Direct selling is the sale of a consumer product or service, person-to-person, away from a fixed retail location, marketed through independent sales representatives who are sometimes also referred to as consultants, distributors or other titles. Estimated 2010 U.S. sales exceed $28 billion.
Source: www.directselling411.com

Direct selling is certainly not a new concept. For years, independent direct sellers have enjoyed the freedom and flexibility of having an independent business. Direct sellers have created their own stories of success by drawing upon their inner motivation and entrepreneurial spirit. Their efforts have led to hundreds of successful companies.

The flavor of direct selling has adapted over the years to respond to the times. In the 1950s and 1960s, party-plan businesses emerged as an outlet for the stereotypical homemaker's need to connect with others. In the 1970s and 1980s, times of fast growth in the direct selling industry, the business provided a viable earning option in an era where women struggled to manage multiple roles. The business provided a way to "have it all." In the 1990s and 2000s, a significant number of new companies, as well as existing consumer brands, entered the direct selling marketplace with high expectations. In the past decade, many of these companies have exited the direct selling channel.

WHAT'S GOING ON IN DIRECT SELLING TODAY?

Today, direct selling aims to respond to the challenges of the times. Direct sellers are looking for new ways to really connect in our increasingly high-tech world. Direct sellers must deal with the reality that women's lives are busier than ever, and that capturing a person's attention is one of today's greatest challenges. The economy is a significant factor in today's selling environment, driving changes in consumer behavior and also in the profile of the typical direct seller. Direct selling is no longer considered to be exclusively a women's business, as an increasing number of men are getting involved.

This is an era of constant access to information, yet many people feel more informed and less inspired than ever. Today, without giving it a second thought, we've trained ourselves to go online for information. We can quickly jet-ski across the surface of website after website, yet it's a rare moment when a web search makes a deep connection with what we're really thinking about and how we're really feeling. And, we don't know what we don't know. Sometimes we're not even clear about what we need or want.

I've witnessed changes in the contemporary direct selling business approach in the work I do as an industry consultant and speaker. Some changes have been subtle. Others have been bold and significant. At times, I wonder if the direct selling industry is facing what many teenagers deal with as they take stock of the characteristics that make them who they are: an identity crisis. Is direct selling about providing consumer information? Is it about social media? Is it about online training? Or, is direct selling more about leveraging the power of human contact to inspire and inform? In this ever-changing environment, it remains to be seen where the industry will go. I remain strong in my belief that selling, real selling, will never go out of style.

HOW DOES SELLING FIT INTO THE PICTURE?

Real selling doesn't happen through your online presence - it happens when you are personally present with people, helping them see possibilities they may have never imagined. While companies today are deepening their efforts in marketing, it's important to consider that marketing is passive. Selling, on the other hand, is active. This isn't a book about online marketing. Or social media. This is a book about the heart of direct selling success — selling.

In this time of significant attention being placed on economy and price, all business professionals benefit when they sharpen the way they talk about their products and services. The words and phrases they choose in their conversations with customers shape perceptions about value. Selling skills are foundational to all areas of business success. Business professionals both inside and outside the direct selling industry tell me that the concepts inside this book have influenced their thoughts and actions, and remain relevant to the work they do each day.

WHAT IS SELLING IT SOFTLY ABOUT?

This book is about the way you think about selling. The way you feel about selling. And, the way you approach what you do when you're selling. With a title like *Selling It Softly*, you may think that this book will recommend a softer, milder approach to managing yourself and your goals. I want to let you in on something that I know to be true: Growing a sales business is a lot of work. The road to selling success is not paved with soft, fluffy feathers. I've noticed something else: Selling, when done well, is worthwhile work. If you could find a way to get more of what you want from your business, isn't that something you could get excited about?

You may be someone who is thinking about the business of direct sales. Or, you may already be in the business and want to grow. Or, maybe you are just curious about the secrets to the highly successful direct sales business model. No matter what inspired you to open this book, I invite you to keep turning the pages. You will read stories that inspire you and instruction that will equip you with actionable ideas to enhance your success.

It is my hope that this book will challenge you to bring your head and your heart to work. That it will stretch the way you think about yourself, your business, and the steps you take each day to create success. That it will leave you feeling inspired, confident, and equipped with what you need to succeed.

If you want more from your selling career — more enjoyment, more earnings, and more experiences — it may be time to explore a softer approach. Create your own story of success. Discover *Selling It Softly*.

INTRODUCTION

CHAPTER | **1**

My Story

When a friend used the word *extraordinary* to describe my career, she meant it as a compliment. Yet it made me feel uncomfortable. I prefer to think of myself as an ordinary woman who worked extremely hard in direct sales. In so doing, I created an extraordinary life, a great income, and opened the door to wonderful choices. And here's the best part: You can, too.

I didn't set out to pursue a life-long career in direct selling. It found me. It was the early 1980's, a time when magazine headlines suggested that a woman had to choose between a life as a career woman or a life as a homemaker. I didn't believe those were the only two options. I was convinced that if I worked hard and stayed focused, I could *have it all*.

I was looking for a flexible way to weave work into my already busy schedule. I knew what was most important to me: something that would work around my family's activities. I wanted new challenges, but not new ways to feel overwhelmed. Work that felt worthwhile. And, of course, work that paid well. I was sure a job like this was waiting for me somewhere. Sure of it.

While the word "entrepreneur" wasn't yet trendy, it had my name all over it. My first venture was to launch a home-based business doing alterations and mending. Once I discovered that I was better at *selling* the work than *doing* the work, I chose to continue my search.

My next venture was a home-based typing business. The clickety-clack of typewriter keys at my dining room table only served to give my three children one more reason to avoid afternoon naps. The search continued.

Next came a weekend job at a local hospital, managing the back-room switchboard in an office the size of a closet. It didn't pay well, but the schedule looked like a good fit. After a few months of working long shifts every Saturday and Sunday, I noticed it was taking a toll on my marriage and family life. The search continued.

A friend and I landed on what we thought would be the answer to our dreams: a crafting business. It didn't take long for us to realize that mass-producing crafts at a dining room table was not a desirable way to generate income. We decided we'd earn more, and enjoy the business more, sharing our creative expertise with others. We launched a small (and short-lived) venture teaching in-home wreath-making classes, but soon discovered we were spending more on supplies than reasonable class tuition could provide. With one more entrepreneurial lesson under my belt, we closed the business. My search continued.

With three boys under the age of two (six-month-old twins and a two-year-old), it was clear that most of what I would earn in a traditional job would be swallowed up in day care bills. More importantly, settling into a traditional work schedule was not what I wanted to do with my life. I wanted to be home for everything as my boys grew up. I wasn't completely sure what *everything* meant, I just knew I wanted to have it all. Wondering if the notion of a balanced work/family life was possible, I thought about accepting a role as a stay-at-home mom and homemaker for the next few years. It felt good to be a wife and mom, and the chaos of being home with three little boys was actually kind of fun.

Still, I needed more going on in my life. Our family was quickly outgrowing our 900-square foot condominium, and we definitely needed more income.

My brain was craving exercise. I happen to enjoy conversations that make me think, and, at the neighborhood playground, I felt like a fish out of water. I worried that if I didn't find something to sink my teeth into, I would resent being home all day while my husband went to work with adults who made him think. My search continued.

I was a twenty-something mom with a busy life, and I was searching for more. The experience of having children has a way of linking us to the lives of our own mothers and grandmothers. My mom had recently died unexpectedly at the age of 52. She was always on my mind and in my heart.

As I spent each day looking for new challenges, I thought about how my mom had spent her life looking for new challenges. Her family needed income, and, at the time, there weren't many job choices for women. She searched for creative ways to earn, and fell back on her sewing skills. As a child, I watched my mom operate her own dress-making business. I remembered saying goodnight to her with bolts of soft, colorful fabric at her side, a hot cup of coffee settling into its familiar groove on the edge of her sewing machine. I would awake the next morning to see bridesmaids' dresses hanging from the handles of the kitchen cupboards.

At a very early age, I learned something that isn't taught in books: There is a connection between *wanting* something and *working for* something. My mom didn't merely put the fabrics next to her sewing machine and go to bed. She worked to create each of those dresses, stitch by stitch.

I am deeply grateful that my mother's work left me with so many life lessons. Modeling is a powerful way of teaching, and my mother's example provided rich opportunities for me to learn about the connection between *want* and *work*, and about believing that you can do the things you set your mind to do. My mom showed me that if you want people to believe in you, you must first believe in yourself.

When I was in the fourth grade, my mother set aside her ribbons and fabrics and ran for public office. She was sure she had what it would take to be elected. *Why not?* . . . she would ask. Not surprisingly, she won the election. Her work called for frequent evening meetings and out-of-town travel. It didn't take long to see that my mom's new career was one of her greatest sources of satisfaction. Her work went on to become so much a part of her life that, at times, I could sense her struggle with the concept of *enough*. My mom had become more at home when she was working than when she was actually at *home*. She worked so much that it didn't leave room for much else in her life.

My experiences as the daughter of a working mom significantly molded my perceptions about what would be important to me as an adult. I imagined my life would include a taste of everything: A satisfying marriage. A fulfilling family life. A challenging career. A warm and inviting home. A big backyard filled with children laughing and playing. And more.

As with many people, direct selling was not my first choice. Intrigued about a company that sold stitchery kits at home parties, I reluctantly signed up as a representative. I found selling, but not success. I was afraid of being pushy, so I was *soft* on myself and even *softer* in my approach to selling. I saw my home parties as a place to teach needlework instead of selling stitchery kits. I thought that by teaching, sales and future business would naturally follow. This passive style led to one more failed attempt at *having it all*. The search continued.

A former business colleague was also looking for a way to balance the satisfaction of a career and the joys of raising a family. While on maternity leave, she decided to enroll in what was then a small start-up company selling kitchen utensils. Curious about what she was doing, I agreed to be one of her first hostesses. I invited my friends and family over to hear about this new company and its exciting collection of kitchen tools that promised to make cooking easier and more fun.

As the sales presentation unfolded in my living room, I thought that this business was something to be excited about. The concept made so much sense. Kitchen stores were few and far between. Cooking was just starting to come back into style. I wanted to be part of this. If I applied myself this time, I knew I would make it. My entrepreneurial sputters had increased my *want* to the point that I was ready to *work*. Best of all, I started the business with a distinct advantage: I knew what *didn't* work.

The next fifteen years of my life were spent selling kitchen tools, working as an independent representative with The Pampered Chef®. I did home shows and recruited and trained others to start businesses, and many of them are still thriving today. I started in sales wanting to work part-time and earn a few hundred dollars a month. My experience as a party plan professional exceeded my expectations. At the end of fifteen years, I had built a team of 1,500 sales representatives who sold a total of $19 Million in kitchen tools in one year. It took ten years of working hard before I earned a six-figure income, and once I achieved that goal, I was pleased that my earnings continued to rise. I earned enough to provide a college education for my three boys and fund a retirement account, and my income matched that of many corporate CEOs. All while experiencing the day-to-day joys of raising my family.

I expected to find new challenges, and I found plenty of them. I expected to be paid well for the work I was doing, and I was. My schedule became less flexible with each passing year, but I remained in control of my calendar. As I learned the business of selling, I worked on learning the business of managing myself. I discovered the difference between managing results and leading people. Along the way, I was surprised to learn much about myself. Success is less about what we *learn* to do and more about what we *decide* to do.

As I look back, I can see my business in three distinct phases. In each phase, I made decisions that opened new opportunities. Let's look at each of them.

PHASE I: GETTING STARTED

The Getting Started phase, for many direct sellers, is not a one-time occurrence, and it certainly wasn't for me. Over the next 15 years, my business started and restarted a number of times.

My first start was the day my husband and I drove our silver Subaru, with the boys in their car seats, to the home of the kitchen company's owner. The owner's husband and mine loaded wooden crates filled with product samples into the trunk. The moment we pulled out of the driveway, I felt like I was officially in business.

During my first startup, I wanted to know how to do everything. At the same time, I wanted to find ways to do everything my own way. I often distracted myself from the heart of what the business really is — selling. It took time to realize that direct selling is about more than *having* a business. It's even about more than *doing* business. What it is really about is *getting* business. I started small, working part-time, scheduling and doing just a few parties each month.

I restarted my business just six months later, when those same wooden crates accompanied me on a family move from Chicago to Minneapolis. I didn't know anyone or anything about Minnesota, I just knew that it had an endless supply of snow. I mailed letters to 100 organizations, inviting their groups to be among the first in the state to host a cooking demonstration with this new, exciting company. I was getting better at getting business. Between follow-up phone calls, and a referral from the company owner, I gathered enough bookings to start again in a new state.

I re-entered the Getting Started phase several more times over the course of my career. Each restart was the result of a self-assessment that nudged me to kick myself out of a slump. Revisiting the startup phase would take me through a process not unlike that of restarting a computer: I would clear out whatever was slowing me down, go back to the starting point, begin with the proper start-up steps, and be ready to function once again. Each restart was a time to dust off product knowledge and refresh my thinking. It was a time to reconnect with early hostesses, revisit the basics of direct selling, and reboot my personal motivation to keep going.

My first few years were rich in learning experiences. Through trial and error, I learned and relearned the fundamental business-building steps: getting parties, doing parties, and recruiting. I discovered the difference between active recruiting and passive recruiting. In my previous life in corporate human resources, I had run newspaper ads to recruit potential employees. I learned that recruiting in direct selling is a different creature. I spent entirely too much money on ads before learning that the best place to recruit is actually the easiest place: at parties. Recruiting is the act of creating interest and the art of personally inviting people to learn about the business. I didn't quite master the art of recruiting in my first five years, but I gained insights which were helpful as I moved to the next stage.

PHASE II: GREEN AND GROWING

In my second five years, my approach to business was less occasional and more intentional. It was time to upgrade my office area from the card table in my laundry room to a real desk in the basement bedroom. Little did I know that a more significant upgrade was on the horizon.

Things were changing at work for my husband. He was facing a common midlife question: *was he doing what he was meant to do with his life?* I remember the day he came home and shared that he was thinking about leaving his corporate job to pursue a career as an elementary school teacher. Only a month earlier, we had moved into a new house, with a much larger mortgage. Now, he wondered if my "little part-time business" could keep our family afloat while he returned to school for a teaching degree. We shared a bottle of wine and figured out that we could make it work. He quit his corporate job to work for me while he went to school.

Everything changed that day. The career transition was a turning point for my husband, for my business, and most of all, for me. For the first time, I needed to step up to the plate and see what I could really do. For the first time, my family was counting on me to become the breadwinner. It was high time I started counting on myself.

I had a choice. I could act as if life changes were happening all around me. Or, I could embrace the new challenges and all that went with them. I turned my focus to growing my business. I became wiser about using my time. I recruited with more intention. My goals became more measurable. I organized more effective team meetings, and more frequent team trainings.

I was doing a lot of recruiting, and training my recruits without the benefit of company training materials. When long-distance team members wanted to learn how to do shows, they struggled to picture how they would cook on a card table in the hostess's living room. Just think about that, it's not easy to explain. I spent a lot of time on the phone walking new team members through how they could cook, sell products, recruit, and create a fun evening for guests all at the same time.

Highly focused on growing my business, I didn't feel like I could wait for the company to reach the point that it would provide comprehensive training materials. So, I created my own. Partnering with a few local team members, we rented a video camera and recorded our own training videos. My husband served as the production manager, camera man, audio technician, and on-location caterer. Between laughs, we recorded how to do a show, setting a boom-box near the microphone to add background music. These training tools were not exactly sophisticated, but they worked. It's important to note that if your company provides materials, this is not a good use of your time. It's better to spend your time with team members as they acquaint themselves with company materials.

People often romance the idea of getting involved with a direct selling company in its early days. There's a false notion that getting in early is the ticket to future success. There were people who enrolled *before* me who didn't stay with the business. There were people who started *after* me who did more with the business than I ever did. There's not a direct connection to when you start and the results you get. Success is more about what you choose to do with your business opportunity once you get going. My experience being involved with a startup company had its challenges. At the same time, the experience of being in at the start opened endless opportunities for me to grow personally, to innovate, and to discover what I was capable of doing.

The Green and Growing Phase was an exciting time for me, for my business, and for my family. My husband and children pitched in to help wherever they were needed, stuffing envelopes and preparing our home for team meetings. It was my business, yet we were all in it together.

My attitudes and actions were forever changed by my husband's entry into his new career, which has led to two decades as a fifth-grade teacher. Fortunately, you won't need your spouse to change careers to experience a turning point. Any day, any way, you can feel a change of heart which leads you to reach for higher levels of business success.

Throughout my career, I noticed how threads of my mother's life became interwoven with mine. My mom had been a career mom long before there were role models. She led the way for countless women, including me, yet no one was there to show her the way or help her know what to watch out for.

In my company, I, too, was on a path which no one had yet been on. I had so many questions. *What should I focus on? How can I get more people like me to join my team? What are the secrets of a successful business? What should I watch out for along the way?* I imagined that a perfect solution would be to spend time with someone a few steps ahead of me on the path to direct selling success.

My company generously arranged a one-on-one meeting for me with a leader from another direct selling company. I couldn't wait to soak up her inspiration and wisdom. We started by talking about our families and our businesses. And then I asked the question. *What are the secrets to maintaining a successful business?* I was surprised by her response.

She asked, *Sue, think about how you'd like to be described. Would you rather hear the words green and growing, or ripe and rotten?* Of course, I made the same choice I suspect you would: green and growing. We spent the rest of our day talking about what it really meant to grow, by recruiting, leading, and building people. I left understanding the value of learning from someone who had been where I wanted to go. I left with a clearer sense of purpose.

With high expectations of my business, I chose to spend a good amount of my time working. You may wonder if I ever felt guilty about taking time away from my husband and children to invest in my business. Of course there were times when I felt guilty. What mother, whether she's working or not, doesn't feel a twinge of guilt taking time for herself at the expense of time with her family? Yet with each passing year I could tell that my sons were learning valuable life lessons. They were learning about the connection between want and work. They were learning about goals. They learned about problem-solving. They watched as I found joy in working. And of course, they knew that my work provided financial benefits for our family. I didn't see my time spent working as a withdrawal from the lives of my family. In more ways than one, my business was a deposit.

Earlier in my career, I had seen recruiting as a way to get what I was looking for: business growth. The more I recruited, the more I realized that recruiting was more effective when I focused less on what I wanted and more on what others wanted. I also discovered it was most satisfying when I thought more about others than I did about myself.

In my pursuit of growth, I was pedaling fast. If you were to describe my style, you might have chosen the word *stressed*. Possibly you would have said *strong*. But probably you wouldn't have used the word *soft*. When *U.S. News and World Report* interviewed me for a cover story about the future of the direct selling industry, they didn't write about how it felt to be successful. They told readers about my business results.

I was awarded my company's Legacy Award of Excellence for my work in developing a strong and successful business model. The award was beautifully presented, and was meant to make me feel honored and appreciated. But at the time, I felt misunderstood. I was frequently described as *business-minded*, *professional*, and *results-oriented*. At first, I thought those were compliments. Over time, however, hearing those words made me start to feel cold and unfeeling. Like I didn't belong in a business where hugs were more commonplace than handshakes.

Each day I learned new things about the art of selling. Yet, I knew that the business was about much, much more than selling kitchen tools. I had embraced the mission of bringing families together around the dinner table, and I had seen countless lives, including my own, change through the experience of direct selling success. While I knew that being a mentor was only part of my role, I was having fun working with people who wanted to grow personally and professionally. As I was discovering the softer side of selling, a softer side of Sue was emerging.

PHASE III: INTENTIONAL DUPLICATION

My decision to build a solid, sustainable business started with thoughts of what I wanted from my business. Over time, I saw that the real rewards were the person I was becoming and the people I had been able to help. I entered my last five years in the field as the leader of a multi-million-dollar team. My husband was enjoying his new career as a fifth grade teacher. Life was good.

Like most direct sellers, I can still remember my first party. My first team meeting. My first incentive trip. I can even remember the first time I ever set foot in a spa and was treated to my first massage.

While all of these personal experiences were meaningful, I knew I felt more significant when I helped others to experience those things. I stepped into a phase of business where I focused on duplicating the experience of success so others could experience it, too.

I worked on the art of setting expectations. I realized that no one starts a direct selling business expecting to fail. I helped team members set an expectation to succeed. And, in the process, I gained skills and confidence.

Analyzing my team's results, I could see that the most successful team members worked consistently. I would share this message with new recruits: *Do one show each week and you will* **have** *a business, do two shows a week and you will* **grow** *your business.* Doing one show a week calls for a time investment that's just 10% of a full-time job. Working less than that, you're not looking at a business, you're looking at an activity. As I would say it to new recruits, I'd remind myself that *success is within the reach of anyone who is willing to work consistently.* With a large team to train and lead, it was getting harder for me to get out and do at least one show a week. However, I knew that if I stopped doing shows, the rest of the team would follow my lead.

Duplication is about looking at yourself and trying to uncomplicate what you do and how you do it. It's easier said than done. In my Intentional Duplication phase, I spent a lot of time thinking about how I could simplify my steps so that others could benefit from my experiences. I studied my approach to recruiting and developed an audio program, *Five Steps To Become a More Remarkable Recruiter.*

I'd love to think that by simplifying the steps I inspired my team members to feel excited about growing their businesses. Okay, maybe the program helped a little, but I don't want to kid myself. Not everyone makes the decision to succeed. Nice people get involved with the business. Fun people. Talented people. Who someone is does not predict their success. It's what they *do*. While most everyone *can* succeed, not everyone chooses to succeed.

The toughest choices I had to make in the Intentional Duplication phase were decisions about where to spend my time. The art of it was investing in people who were investing in themselves. I learned to separate being friendly from being a person's friend. While this sounds like an easy thing to do, I found it to be one of the hardest things to learn.

I particularly enjoyed working with Leaders and team members who wanted to be Leaders. I worked to find a balance between helping them build skills while also helping them be independent. I wanted each Leader to trust her instincts the way I came to trust mine, knowing that tough learning experiences are often the ones which build the most confidence. I held quarterly business assessment calls with each Leader, asking them to come to calls with a form showing their measurable results in personal sales, recruiting, and team building. They didn't love having to look up all of their numbers to prepare for a call, but they appreciated being nudged to take stock of their business growth. The calls gave us a time to strategize and celebrate together.

I received several awards for developing my team, and I have to admit it was fun to earn recognition for things I was going to do anyway. Yet what I enjoyed more than receiving recognition was giving recognition. I loved creating ways for team members to stand up and bask in the praise of their peers. I noticed that over the years they had started to stand a little taller. Their successes made my work worthwhile.

THE NEXT CHAPTER

At the end of fifteen years, I was at the top of my game. I believed I could do whatever I set out to do. I had accomplished everything I wanted to do, and more. It felt like it was time to turn in my apron and try a new role in direct selling. Turning away from a $19 Million business and the income that took so much time and work to build was a tough decision. A really tough decision. The thing was, I was still an entrepreneur with a heart for new ventures.

That was my experience. Yours may be different. My decision considered three primary factors:

• **Income.** I was earning more than I had ever imagined, and money was no longer a big motivator. Very early in my career, my husband and I hired a financial planner to help us make the most of our earnings (we took this step before there were many earnings to make the most of). With his help, we created structure and discipline to build college savings funds, a rainy-day fund, and a retirement fund. In my mind, there was a big red check mark next to my family financial goals. So, no issue there.

• **Energy.** There's a common misconception about direct sales. Some think that you build it big, then you earn big as you sit there and admire your success. I have seen many give that approach a try, although I've never seen it lead to sustainable success. To succeed in direct sales you must keep going and you must keep growing. I had noticed that too much of my energy was going into searching for enthusiasm. I was growing tired. At times I would look into my own eyes and see my mother, who struggled with the concept of *enough.* The time had come for me to say it out loud: ***enough.***

• **Challenge.** I was busy all day, yet I was bored. I started a **List of 100**, a hand-written compilation of things I wanted to do in my life. Some were big, some were small. I still have that list. It's in a red folder in my desk drawer, filed under G for Goals. It falls right behind the last file in the F section, *Funerals*. In the timeline of my life, I hope those two fall in a different order.

I took inventory of my list, and noticed a couple of things. Some of the items had been accomplished numerous times. I also noticed that my list had a number of career-related challenges. For many people, daily thoughts center on the things in life that work makes possible. There's a lot that's wonderfully right about that way of thinking. Yet I am wired to find challenges not only outside of work, but also *within* work.

I watched my husband as he made his midlife decision to leave business for the classroom. Now that his career was underway, I wondered if it was my turn. I was in my 40's, and I didn't want to wait too long to figure out if I had another career in me.

I am grateful for what the experience brought to my life and to the lives of my family. The journey had been worthwhile. One of my sons, then a teenager, validated this for me when he wrote:

Your business has made an impact in my life. I have learned a lot about cooking, about business, about hard work and about boring work. I've learned about goal-setting and accomplishing. I am very happy you have done something you liked.

Ironically, the very elements of my character which had helped me create a successful business were now calling me to leave it behind and explore other avenues. My experience brought me income, skills, and resources that made it possible to make new choices. I wanted to create a new experience, something of my own, that I could sink my teeth into. A little scared, a lot excited, and filled with anticipation, I started a new business that combined my skills and interests with a real need in the marketplace.

I reinvented myself. I didn't see a job anywhere that felt right to me, so I created one. I became a business consultant and speaker. My past *getting started* experiences served me well as I created my potential client list. I made phone calls one at a time until I developed my first clients. It took time for my new business to develop, but life lessons and past experiences had taught me that I could do whatever I set my mind to. I went on to work with companies at all stages of development, from early start-ups through seasoned companies looking to reinvigorate their sales forces. Some of the companies which I had once admired from a distance were now companies I was proud to serve as a consultant and strategic advisor.

As I was building my consulting skills, I was also doing a great deal of speaking. I traveled around the U. S. and Canada, sharing strategies that had contributed to my success as a direct selling leader. The more I spoke, the more my client list grew. I met thousands of people, and I enjoyed seeing how direct selling was making a difference in their lives.

After seven years of working for myself, my career opened another door. One of my consulting clients was Crayola®, a division of Hallmark. In 2005, they were looking for a Vice President to lead a recently-launched direct sales division called Big Yellow Box by Crayola®. I imagined one of the most-loved brands coming to life in homes across the country, and I could see endless possibilities. I'd been working solo for seven years, and I missed the camaraderie of working with a team. When Crayola® invited me to leave my independent business to lead this new startup division, I took a big gulp and accepted the challenge.

The Crayola® sales force had been selling for 15 months when I stepped in to lead the division, and the culture had already started to take shape. Expectations were high, both in the field and in the corporate offices. The company made a significant investment in the success of this division. Each Monday morning — I had 100 of them over the next two years — I looked ahead to a week of unanswered questions, and the toughest was: *Where will I direct my time this week to grow the business?* The answers weren't always clear and the challenges were many.

I discovered that financial backing is just one factor which can contribute to a company's success, and often not the most important factor. A company's success begins with a product that's so compelling it creates a viral response. Success continues when a significant number of recruits enroll and embrace the belief that their success will be tied to more than brand equity — their success will be tied to their consistent activity in selling, recruiting, and training. It takes a long time to cultivate a field culture which places a high value on party productivity and recruiting consistency.

Despite the significant efforts of many who worked tirelessly to deliver success, our business results did not rise quickly enough to meet expectations. While Big Yellow Box by Crayola® was a short-lived venture, in my mind it was a meaningful effort. The business of sharing creativity touched numerous lives, including my own. I consider my time at Crayola® to be one of the most colorful experiences of my life.

Being a self-employed sales professional isn't easy. Yet, wouldn't you agree . . . the things in life that are easy are rarely the things in life worth having? I have returned to consulting for companies and sales professionals who want to experience more success. I enjoy being in a business where people grow personally as they grow professionally. I've come to realize that selling success is less about anything you *get*, and more about the person you *become* through the experience.

Of course, mine is not the only story of direct selling success. Perhaps you, a neighbor, sister, or friend have a success story. As I've shared, I feel a little uncomfortable when people describe what I've done as extraordinary. Again, I am an ordinary woman who worked extremely hard in direct sales, and in so doing, I created an extraordinary life.

I know that you can do what I've done. My hope is that *Selling It Softly* will help you create your own story of success. May you enjoy every step of your journey.

RETHINKING THE ART OF SELLING

RETHINKING THE ART OF SELLING

It's unusual to see the words *emotion* and *business* in the same sentence. Yet direct sales professionals know that this is a business that calls for feeling as much as thinking.

Selling is an art. Part of what keeps it interesting is that there is not a proven cookie-cutter approach that works for everyone. The most effective direct sellers know the obvious: in a people business, part of the art is in how they connect with other people. They also know that to succeed they must show up being just one person: themselves.

In this section we look at how to tune in to what our customers really want and need. We will take a well-rounded look at what you sell, exploring four questions to identify what matters most about your products. We will look at elements of your style, and how you can cultivate a soft-selling style which is truly your own. Let's rethink the art of selling.

CHAPTER | 2

What Customers Want and Need

Do customers chase you down and beg you to sell them your products? Doubtful. Selling is more than the art of *responding* to interest which comes your way. Selling is about *igniting* interest in people who may not know they need, or want, what you have to offer.

When I was selling, never once did I hear someone say, *Sue, I woke up knowing that today is THE day I need to go shopping for a garlic press.* Yet, after many sales presentations, I heard customers tell me they didn't think they could live another day without a good garlic press. What's the difference? Selling. As sales professionals, we're in the business of inspiring customers to connect with the life-enhancing benefits of what we have to offer.

Sometimes we learn the most about selling when we're on the buying side. I was treated to an unexpected learning experience when I decided to remodel my kitchen. I invited several professionals to come to my home to give me quotes. The first remodeler made it clear that he would only take a few minutes to write a quote. He asked me to describe exactly what I was looking for as he took measurements. I was disappointed when the second remodeler also wanted me to describe the specifics of the project — that's what I wanted him to do. I was distracted by his multi-tasking as we talked about what was important to me: my kitchen. The first two remodelers provided very specific quotes summarizing the way they'd remodel my kitchen to match the specifications I described.

And then I met Peter, the third remodeling professional. Peter warmly shook my hand and smiled as he introduced himself. I instantly noticed his deep wrinkles, which suggested that this guy was at the edge of retirement. I wondered how important my project would be to him at this stage of the game. *I'm Peter*, he said, *I'm pleased to meet you.* He pointed out the obvious. *I bet you are wondering what an old guy like me is still doing in a business like this. You see, I retired about five years ago. I missed working with people like you who are ready to make your home into exactly what you want it to be . . . so I'm back. I look forward to talking with you today about your kitchen.* I was right. This guy was at the edge of retirement. Just not the edge I had expected.

I am almost six feet tall. As we stood in the entryway, I towered over Peter, who couldn't have been more than five feet tall. I invited him into the kitchen and we passed the collection of family photos in the entryway. He stopped to ask a few questions about each of my sons, and paused to say, *Great looking family!* This guy was talking my language. My needs assessment speech was quite well-polished after talking to the other remodelers, so I jumped right in and started talking. Peter listened as I rattled on, and when I came up for air, he interjected, *Sue, would it be ok if I asked a few questions about YOU, before we talk about your kitchen?* I was really starting to like this guy. I loved the thing about coming back after retirement. The questions about my boys connected to the heart of what matters most to me. And now, he wanted to make our conversation all about me. What's not to like?

He asked, *so can you take a few minutes to tell me the ways that this kitchen is coming up short?* (I suspected that he may have grown accustomed to using the word "short. ") He didn't want to hear the solutions I had already come to — he wanted to know about the problems I knew about. Then he asked, *Have you thought about building your countertops a little higher? As I looked at your family photos, I noticed that you seem to grow them pretty tall around here.* He suggested that I build my counters six inches higher so that instead of having to lean over to reach the counter tops, my kitchen counters would rise up to meet me.

He asked if I had ever considered a salad sink. I answered, *Well, yes, I make salads – and when I do, I use a sink. I'm not sure I need a special sink, though. What is it for?* He told me that it was an extra sink that would make it easier for more than one person to work in the kitchen at once. Just think about the imagery he created with this idea. Does it lead you to picture yourself in your kitchen with other people?

Peter shared ideas I hadn't considered. We don't know what we don't know. Peter helped me think about how it would feel to have a kitchen that I loved. At the end of our consultation, I sent Peter on his way with a generous deposit check. And, by the way, it was a great choice to elevate the countertops and install my much-loved salad sink.

So, what does all of this mean to you? Whether you sell in a person-to-person setting, a group environment, or both, there's a lot to learn from Peter. He asked questions to make the buying experience personal. He sold to more than my functional needs – he connected with my emotional needs. He helped me see my kitchen in a way that I hadn't seen it before.

No matter what your title is, your role in direct selling is to sell your company's products and services. Would you like to bring a soft-selling style into your work? As we rethink what it really means to sell, let's take a look at what distinguishes a sales professional from a product demonstrator.

PRODUCT DEMONSTRATOR	SALES PROFESSIONAL
Focuses on the product	Focuses on the people
Emphasizes features	Emphasizes feelings
Shows what a product can do	Shows how it matters

Demonstrating products isn't a bad thing to do. It's just that if you want to succeed in selling, demonstrating products isn't enough. Soft sellers inspire interest and illuminate value. Whether you sell to individuals or groups, part of what will make you successful is the extent to which you connect with emotion.

Wouldn't it be great if customers were already interested in what you have to sell at the time you started talking with them? If you're in party-plan sales, you know that this is not always the case. Guests usually know more about the hostess or other guests than they do about your business. If someone does know a few things about your company or your products, she may have a preconceived notion about whether she wants or needs what you have to share. By the way, have you ever had a guest take a moment before the sales presentation to offer a "heads up" that she's not really in the market for what you're about to present? It's as if she needs to create an out before she even hears what you have to say. Interestingly, I've found such guests often go on to become enthusiastic customers.

As a sales professional, you will illustrate possibilities which your customers may never have considered before, like the salad sink.

The first step to doing this well is to raise your awareness about what customers need, and what customers really want. What do customers think is important? What wants do they bring to the selling process?

A desire to save time
Busy is the new normal. No matter what walk of life your customers are in, it is common to hear people say they have a lot going on. People want more time, whether it's time to get more done, or time to relax and celebrate the things which have been done.

A desire to save money
In the current decade, people are paying more attention than ever to how they spend. Whether or not they face economic struggles, messages about the dollar surround them constantly. It has actually become fashionable to be economical

Let's think of the desire to save time, and the desire to save money, as known wants — things people talk openly about. Add other needs to this list which relate specifically to the products you sell. Real selling happens when you help customers see your products and services as a way to get more of what they want and need. No matter what you are selling, you will make more connections when you also focus on your customers' emotional needs. Let's look:

The need to feel appreciated
Like all of us, your customers go through life each day wanting to know they are appreciated. Whether they care for a home or a family, or they go to a job each day, does life deliver the amount of applause they want and need? How could your products put more applause into their lives? When you talk about your products, to what extent do you help them see that

using your products may lead to the appreciation they really deserve? For example, if you are selling gourmet food, could your products help someone get lots of appreciation at home or at work for making a spectacular dish?

The need to appreciate others

Do people go around saying that they are looking for ways to appreciate others? Not often. Yet the pace of life may be keeping your customers from the joy of showing appreciation. Do your products help customers appreciate others? If so, in what ways? When you speak about your products, to what extent do you invite them to connect with this need? For example, if you sell products to create hand-made cards, do you offer customers a special way to express appreciation to others? If you sell personalized gifts, do your products give the customer a way to say *thank you* to teachers, coaches, or child care providers?

The need to realize a dream

When life is busy, it's hard to make time for dreaming. It is a rare day that a customer enters a sales presentation with her life's dreams at the top of her mind. If you ask someone what she needs, she is more likely to say she needs a massage or a latte than to talk about the depth of a dream. When Peter stepped into my kitchen, he helped me see that I knew how to dream. My dream was my family sitting around the kitchen table enjoying togetherness. Having a kitchen that truly felt like home. When you are working with your customers, what dreams do your products help them realize? In what ways do your products help them realize those dreams?

The need to belong

Few people will readily admit that they would like a stronger sense of belonging. Yet for most of us, there's a need to feel that we are part of something bigger than ourselves. That we matter. We want to feel that a get-together would not have been the same if we hadn't been there. Do your products connect with your customers' need to belong? If so, how? To what extent do you connect with that unspoken emotional need during your sales presentation? For example, if you're selling photograph storage products, how do your products remind customers that they are an important and essential part of their family? If you're selling the invitation to be part of your team, how do you connect with a customer's desire to be part of your group?

The need to feel in control

Many customers feel more peace and comfort when they believe they're managing their daily choices and schedules. In what ways do your products create a feeling of command over one's time? To what extent do you talk about this emotional need as you share your products? For example, if you're selling skin care systems, how do they streamline the customer's morning routine? If you're selling fashion products, how do they make the customer feel more in control of daily wardrobe decisions?

The need to connect

We have more devices than ever to contact each other, yet many of us still have a deep need to foster real connections with other people. How do your products bring people together? Does the experience your company provides invite connections with friends and family? How often do you use the word *connect* during your sales presentation? For example, if you're selling toys and books, do you emphasize the feeling of connection as you show the products? If you're selling the opportunity to host a home show, do you stress the joy of connecting with friends and acquaintances?

The need to be noticed
Some people draw energy from group situations when they feel they stand out. Can the experience of using your products inspire a compliment? In what ways? To what extent do you help your customers imagine themselves being noticed as a result of using your products? For example, if you sell jewelry, do you help the customer imagine herself receiving compliments for how great she looks?

The idea of talking about deep emotional needs during the sales process may feel a little *out there* to you. Later, we will look at how to make subtle shifts, one at a time. At this point, we are looking at the concept of putting more heart into the business of selling. We're rethinking the art of selling.

While we are thinking about art, let's take a moment to consider what it means to create an image. One of Norman Rockwell's most recognized works, *Freedom From Want*, is a memorable image of a grandmother bringing a perfectly-cooked golden turkey to the Thanksgiving table. Grandpa is reaching for the carving set so he can follow the appropriate *oohs* and *aahs* with the traditional act of carving the turkey tableside. You can't help but notice the warmth and love around the table in an image created by this skillful artist. Everyone is smiling. When you see this image, you are drawn into the loving connections around the table. There's a palpable feeling of *home*.

When you're selling, you use words to paint pictures in the minds and hearts of your customers. To choose words that connect, it's important to keep your customers' needs and wants in the forefront. Deep down, does your customer want the feeling of being around that family Thanksgiving table? Does she have an unspoken desire to be noticed for her uniqueness? What is your customer really looking for? What does she want? What does she need?

Let's explore how you can ignite interest in people who may not know they need, or want, what you have to offer. If you're looking for more sales, and you want your work to feel more significant, it may be time to rethink your approach. It may be time to start *Selling It Softly*.

CHAPTER | 3

What You Sell and Why it Matters

You've considered the difference between being a demonstrator and being a sales professional. You have thought about what matters to your customer. It's likely that you are already familiar with the idea of distinguishing your product's features from its benefits:

- *Features* are facts which describe what a product is and what it does.

- *Benefits* speak to the value a product has for the buyer.

As we continue to explore the art of selling, let's build upon the basic concept that features and benefits play different roles in selling conversations. In this chapter we will look at four questions to refresh your thinking about the products you sell.

ASSUMPTIONS

We will journey through this section with the following assumptions:

- You have a heart for what you sell, or you wouldn't have chosen to sell it.

- Your intention is to sell more products so you can help more people enjoy the life-enhancing benefits of what you have to offer.

- The same skills you use to sell products will be used to sell other services, programs, or opportunities.

A well-rounded look
at what you sell

VALUE
What makes it matter?

FUNCTIONAL BENEFITS
What does it do?

EMOTIONAL BENEFITS
What feelings does it create?

What is it?

FEATURES

©2012 Sue Rusch

What we're about to explore is a new way of looking at the products you sell. We'll look at four questions to ask yourself as you rethink your products and services.

This is not a step-by-step selling system. It's a way of thinking about what you sell and how you sell it.

A well-rounded look at what you sell

VALUE
What makes it matter?

FUNCTIONAL BENEFITS
What does it do?

EMOTIONAL BENEFITS
What feelings does it create?

What is it?

FEATURES

©2012 Sue Rusch

FEATURES

What is it?

Think about one of your best-selling products. What are its physical features? Which words would you choose to describe that product?

- What material is it made of?
- What is its size?
- Is it soft?
- Is it heavy?
- Is it sturdy?

- What color is it?
- Is it smooth?
- Is it textured?
- Is it fragrant?
- Is it flavorful?

What is it? Your customers expect you to know your products, don't they? Your confidence and product knowledge builds their trust in you as the salesperson. However, it is not necessary to memorize the specific details of every item in your catalog. In fact, if you're in party-plan sales, you know you're also modeling the Consultant role. You don't want to come across as a walking encyclopedia with every factoid about a product on the tip of your tongue. This might make your job look complicated.

As you reach for words to describe the physical features of your product, you may feel uninspired. Dimensions, materials, and design characteristics rarely create excitement.

Let's put this first question, *What is it?* into perspective. Here, we are choosing words to describe the physical product. For example, you might describe the material that a piece of jewelry is made of. You may say that the garment you are showing is made of cotton. You might state that the paper you are showing is acid-free.

Later, we'll draw a distinction between physical features and life-enhancing benefits. *What is it?* is just the first of four questions to ask as you rethink your products.

Now, let's look at what your product can do.

A well-rounded look
at what you sell

VALUE
What makes
it matter?

EMOTIONAL BENEFITS
What feelings does it create?

FUNCTIONAL BENEFITS
What does it do?

What is it?

FEATURES

©2012 Sue Rusch

FUNCTIONAL BENEFITS

What does it do?

As you think about that best-selling product, consider its functionality. Let's imagine you are selling a Bread Mix and speaking about the product's basic function.

> *This Bread Mix, blended with a few ingredients, makes a fresh loaf of bread.*

What does it do? . . . The second of the four questions leads you to think about your product's function. Showing a product's versatility during the selling process is one way to elevate perceived value. The more ideas you share, the grander the possibilities you introduce, and the more you increase the product's appeal.

What does it do? Let's go back to our Bread Mix example, and show some more uses:

> *This Bread Mix, blended with a few ingredients, makes a fresh loaf of bread. And... did you know that this bread mix also makes a quick and easy pizza crust? You will love having this product in your pantry — it's so versatile!*

When you talk about functional benefits, you are opening your customers' minds to new possibilities. You are showing how much one product can do. A great way to introduce product versatility is to invite customers to share ideas with each other.

The more that customers believe a product can do, the higher its perceived value will be . . . and the more likely they'll buy. For example, if you're selling a tray, your customers will be delighted to see that it doubles as a beautiful wall decoration. If you're selling jewelry, they'll enjoy seeing different ways to wear one necklace. You get the idea.

Soft-selling is the art of rising above the physical features in all that you do and say. It's helping your customers explore life-enhancing benefits.

Now, let's get to the
real heart of the *soft-selling* style.

A well-rounded look
at what you sell

VALUE
What makes
it matter?

EMOTIONAL BENEFITS

What
feelings
does it
create?

FUNCTIONAL BENEFITS

What does
it do?

What
is it?

FEATURES

©2012 Sue Rusch

EMOTIONAL BENEFITS

What feelings does it create?

While functionality plays a supporting role in creating inspiration, emotion plays the starring role. In the third of our four questions, we stretch beyond features and functional benefits. Here, we start to use the language of emotion, looking at how a product meets the customer's wants and needs. Here, we focus less on what the product is, and more on how it *feels* to use it.

Bring stories of satisfied customers into your sales presentation. For example, you might share a story of how a customer felt more confident wearing jewelry. Or share a customer's experience with giving your product as a gift. Let people know how you feel about your products. Most of all, invite customers to picture your product in their hands and in their lives. Invite them to imagine how your product will make them *feel*.

What feelings does it create? Let's look at a concrete example. Imagine you are selling a photo album.

What is it?
A sturdy 8 x 10 cloth-covered book made of acid-free paper, with interchangeable pages and a variety of accessories.

What does it do?
Preserves photographs, journaling, and mementoes effectively, safely, and creatively.

What feelings does it create?
• A feeling of connection to other people and past life experiences.
• A feeling of pride in creative expression.
• A feeling of joy in celebrating life's moments.

This shows the difference between what something *is* and what it *can be*. Can you see how these three questions moved our thinking about the product from its features to its functionality to its feelings? Think about how you can take your products from being hard things that customers hold to products with soft benefits.

Your customers don't just think, they feel. Emotion is an essential ingredient in soft-selling success, and it is one that distinguishes the direct selling style from retail or business selling.

Now, let's understand the real value of the products you sell.

A well-rounded look
at what you sell

VALUE

What makes
it matter?

FUNCTIONAL BENEFITS

What does
it do?

EMOTIONAL BENEFITS

What
feelings
does it
create?

What
is it?

FEATURES

©2012 Sue Rusch

VALUE

What makes it matter?

Value is the relationship between the price and the perceived worth of a product or service. To help your customer see the real value of what you sell, share how the product can enhance her life. Our previous questions led us to consider the fourth question, ***What makes it matter?*** Here, we focus less on price and more on value.

- What experiences will be possible in the customer's life as the result of your product?

- Can a price be placed on those experiences?

- What makes your product relevant today?

- What makes this season a good time to consider what you're selling?

- What do satisfied customers often tell you about why this product matters to them?

What makes it matter? Can you think of a time when you felt you absolutely, positively had to make a particular purchase?

- Was it when you tried on those bright red shoes and pictured yourself making a bold statement at your high school reunion? In that moment, did you pay attention to the price tag?

- Was it when you walked into your house and felt it would become your home? In that moment, did you even care that the house didn't have the three-car garage you originally saw as a must-have?

When we become emotionally connected to a product, we no longer make decisions using logic. The minute we imagine our lives with that product, we step into feeling mode. When the product becomes relevant to us and to our lives, we see its value. How can your products help people get what really matters to them? In this fourth question about value, we're connecting back to your customer's unspoken needs.

If you have encountered price resistance, ask yourself:

- Have I been spending too much time on what the product does instead of how it makes them feel?

- Have I spent enough time on life-enhancing value?

- What could happen if I focused more on getting customers excited about what matters to them?

A well-rounded look at what you sell

VALUE — What makes it matter?

EMOTIONAL BENEFITS — What feelings does it create?

FUNCTIONAL BENEFITS — What does it do?

What is it?

FEATURES

©2012 Sue Rusch

As we explored each of the four questions, you may have noticed something: the questions aren't numbered. That's because you're not looking at a new selling system, or a new step-by-step process. You're looking at a way to rethink what you sell.

There's no one single starting point. There will be times when you start with a value-related comment, then introduce a specific product and all that it can do. Other times, you will start by connecting with a feeling, then show a product's function as you share features your customer is looking for.

Revisit these four questions often as you rethink everything you sell:

- Your products

- Your company

- Your home party experience

- Add-on services

- Your business opportunity

When you think differently about what you sell, your soft-selling style will naturally evolve.

CHAPTER | 4

A Softer Style

Your style is the way you do what you do. A soft-selling style is collaborative and engaging. When you're in the business of selling, you're *not* in the business of impressing people. You're in the business of making connections with the way people think and feel. Imagine yourself in a coffee shop, having a conversation with a friend. Are you smiling? Are you relaxed? Are you just being yourself? That person you just saw — *you* — is the best person to bring to your sales presentations. A style that's comfortable, relaxed, and authentic.

Let's look at four elements of the soft-selling style, and how they add up to selling success.

❶ Sales Professional as facilitator

You are not selling *to* people, you are selling *with* people. You'll have more fun when it's not all about you, and so will your customers. An effective soft-selling style is less about *presenting*, and more about *involving*. Master the art of engaging your audience.

One way to involve customers is to ask questions. In a group setting, many of your questions will be rhetorical. You're not looking for hands to shoot up as if you're in a classroom. Ask questions to provoke thoughts and feelings. For example, you might ask, *how would you feel using something like this every day? ... or ... For you, what would be the best part about sharing something like this with your family?* You get the idea. Invite customers to do more than think. Inspire them to feel.

Part of what makes group selling effective is that you invite people to share insights and experiences with each other. Customer comments have more impact than any statements you can make. Party plan professionals know that the hostess is an important partner in the success of the party experience for everyone. Shine a light on the hostess and allow her to be the star of the show. Invite her to share what is important to her. She wants to connect with her friends and family, and, as a facilitator, you help make that happen. The more engaged everyone is, the more compelling the experience will be. So, what this means to you is more fun, more sales, and more future business.

❷ Sales Professional who shares information and ideas

How do you learn about the products you sell? By using them! Personal experience with products leads to new stories and questions for your sales presentation. If it has been awhile since you've enjoyed a particular product, it may be time to dust it off so you can refresh your experience. As you use a product, ask yourself how it feels. Fall in love with your own products so you can help others get excited about them, too.

❸ Sales Professional as enthusiastic consumer

Meet your customer where she is. We're not talking about your geographical meeting place, we're talking about the manner in which you connect. When I was selling kitchen tools, I occasionally met a professional chef with an interest in becoming a consultant. At first glance, you might think a person with professional chef's training would be a natural. However, I discovered that sellers who position themselves as experts are often less effective at making emotional connections than sellers who position themselves as enthusiastic consumers. Let's compare the two:

Expert positioning: *I am a proven expert in the area of fashion. I am here to share my vast knowledge and experience with you tonight. I'll be showing you how to accessorize and update your wardrobe, and I will be teaching you what I know about the importance of dressing with style.*

Enthusiastic consumer positioning: *In many ways, I am like you. I face the same challenges you do when it comes to deciding what to wear each day — I know how it feels. When I discovered our company, I saw for myself what a big difference our easy-to-wear fashions make in life each day ... for me, and for many others. Whether you are already acquainted with our clothes and accessories, or you're learning about them for the first time, I can't wait to share this experience with you tonight. We're going to have a good time!*

Do you see how positioning yourself as an enthusiastic consumer connects with the customer where she is?

❹ Sales Professional who sets the tone

As you drive to your next sales presentation, ask yourself, *what are the customers I am about to meet doing right now?* It's possible that your guests are relaxing as they anticipate the home party experience, but it's not likely. When they arrive at the party, they will need you to set the tone for fun and interaction. Greet them warmly as they arrive. Engage them in conversation to set the tone for interaction. Most importantly, remember to bring your smile.

Up to now, you may have thought that selling is selling, whether you are selling a car in a showroom, a consumer product in a retail store, or you're selling business-to-business to a CEO in her office. The direct selling environment is in a home — the warmest environment possible. When you sell in homes, a soft style is a better fit than a professional, polished business approach. Let's take a look at some of the ways in which direct selling distinguishes itself from other forms of selling:

Process: Direct selling is less about prospecting for people who need what you sell, and more about building relationships with people who will lead you to others. In group selling, people gather for a social experience first, and a selling experience second. In direct selling, relationships are central to success.

Decision-making: Direct sellers usually interact directly with one decision-maker. Buying decisions are typically made on-the-spot in response to information, inspiration, and the fun of shopping in the company of friends and family. You're not responding to a formal request for proposal, and you're not selling to a decision-making committee.

Price: The direct selling approach minimizes price resistance by emphasizing a product's life-enhancing value. Customers consider purchasing things which they may have never even looked at in a retail environment, which often eliminates the comparative price mindset.

Competition: A smart soft-selling style includes few, if any, references to competitors. The seller aims to attract people who want to do business with her, not repel people from doing business with others.

Emotion: In direct selling, much of the selling style is about connecting with the heart. Direct selling is less about facts and more about feelings.

As you can see, the soft style of direct selling distinguishes itself as very different from the style of other forms of selling. So what does this mean to you? The direct selling style isn't *better*. It isn't *more than*, it isn't *less than*. It's just *different*. A soft-selling style calls for active use of your head and your heart.

So, while we're talking about a selling style that's soft, we are still talking about selling. You may have heard it said that *good products sell themselves*. When I hear that, I think to myself, *really*? Have you ever seen your products smile? Have you ever heard a product ask great questions to bring people together? I doubt it. That's what *you* do. At times you may have felt as though your products sell themselves. Instead, think about how important you are to the success of your business, and respect the work you do. Feel excited as you develop your own soft style of selling.

**How to put more of yourself
into your sales presentations:**
- Be a facilitator
- Share information and ideas
- Position yourself as an enthusiatic consumer
- Set the tone and remember to smile

SAYING IT SOFTLY

SAYING IT SOFTLY

You want more customers to buy products, schedule parties, and meet with you to learn about your products and business opportunity. You're looking for the right words to inspire action, but but you don't want to be viewed as *pushy*.

STORIES TO INSPIRE YOU

A powerful story can bring your product to life. Story-telling, combined with the art of asking effective questions, can stir a customer's interest in taking action. You are about to experience ten stories from various stages of my life's journey. Each is written to provoke thought and emotion, and to prepare you to learn a series of ten *story-starter* phrases.

INSTRUCTION TO EQUIP YOU

Each story is followed by instruction pages to equip you with ways to weave new phrases into your selling vocabulary. The instruction pages offer specific examples using a variety of products. You may even recognize an example that uses products similar to yours. These examples are provided for illustration, and to inspire you to create your own style.

It is likely that your company provides recommended selling scripts that show you how to bring your products to life. The concepts in this section are not intended to replace your company's sales training. They're presented to expand your selling vocabulary, and to elevate the way you present the benefits of your products and services. Direct sellers sell more than products, so the instruction pages also include illustrations of the *story-starter* phrases in use in conversations with potential hosts and prospective team members.

**Experience the stories. Experience the learning.
Experience ... *saying it softly*.**

SOMETIMES, WHEN YOU'RE SELLING . . .

. . . you want to help your customer

Imagine

Opens the door to discuss concerns.

Let's look at a story.

CHAPTER | 5

Imagine

Put your customer at the center of her own story.

On my office shelf is a treasured gift: wooden letters which spell out the word *Imagine*. This one word inspires me to create rich and colorful images, ideas, and possibilities.

It was an exciting time when we started shopping for our first house. My husband had just accepted a job in Minnesota, and our tiny Chicago condominium was almost ready to go on the market. At the time, with three children under the age of three, our limited childcare options suggested a very short Minneapolis house-hunting trip. We created a detailed list of everything we were looking for in our new home.

With a long wish list and short timeframe, our realtor arranged an action-packed day of twelve showings. Like many first-time homeowners, budget limitations were a big factor in our decision. After just a few showings, we realized we'd have to revisit our detailed list and make some choices. We'd need to choose a home farther from the city and settle for a longer commute, or we'd have to settle on a closer home that was smaller. With only half a day of looking yet to go, our enthusiasm was fading.

There was something very ordinary, yet quite inviting, about the green house on Kell Avenue South. Walking to the front door around a curved sidewalk, we stepped gingerly over chalk artwork and the pull-string of a small toy wagon. I imagined that bright red wagon in the hands of one of my sons. In my mind's eye, I could see three little boys scribbling their names, and more, all over that sidewalk.

The moment we stepped through the front door, though, I stopped feeling and started thinking. Logic crept in. It was as if I was holding a clipboard, a pencil resting in the crook of my ear, and I was ready to check off what did not measure up. No foyer. Orange carpet. Dark woodwork. Small bedrooms.

Our realtor invited me to the back of the house to see the kitchen. Bright sunshine gleamed through a generous bay window. The view out the kitchen window was inviting. Tired of condominium living, I immediately fell in love with the backyard. I could picture myself sipping a hot cup of morning coffee, hearing laughter as my boys played in the yard. I just stood there. I took it all in. I *imagined*.

When our realtor asked if I could see my family at that kitchen table next to the bay window, I smiled. That day, that moment, I imagined my life in that house. For many happy years, our family loved calling the light green house with the inviting back yard our home.

CONCEPT OVERVIEW

Can you imagine yourself at the bay window, looking out at your family? *Imagine*. It's a powerful word. When you are selling, you help your customer picture herself living her life enjoying your product.

Imagine works well in the selling process when you start talking before you pick up your product. Invite your customer to picture an everyday situation or setting. With her, explore what she might want or need in that particular setting. Use words as your paintbrush and create a mental image. Help the customer see herself at the center of the story. Help her know how it feels to need what you're about to share. Only then will you reach for your product, and lead her to imagine herself enjoying and appreciating the product. First, set the stage with your *Imagine* story. Then, introduce the product as a solution.

Many of us process thoughts by converting them to visual pictures. It's the same way a child processes a thought as she listens to a storybook. The child listens carefully to each word you say. As she hears your words, she looks at the colorful pictures. She … imagines. This is what we do when we use *imagine* to tell stories in the selling process. The difference is that instead of showing a picture, we invite customers to create their own pictures.

YOU CAN SAY …

- *Imagine* …
- Can you picture …
- Think of how it would feel to …

Let's look at some examples of this concept in action …

EXAMPLES

EXAMPLE #1: *You're selling gourmet food*

Imagine, it's a Saturday morning and everyone else is still in bed. You put on a pot of coffee, and sit down to start the crossword puzzle. You think, *aahhh, this is not an ordinary Saturday. How great is this, there is NOTHING on the calendar!* **Imagine**, how would that feel? You open your pantry and right there, smiling up at you, is our Baking Mix. You decide that today's the day you'll create a special breakfast. Imagine your family's faces as they step into the kitchen and smell the aroma of those special rolls. Just this one mix, and you can turn an ordinary Saturday into an extraordinary memory. Wouldn't you agree, it's delicious moments like these that we savor?

EXAMPLE #2: *You're selling skin care*

Can you think of how it would feel to look into the mirror on your bathroom wall, and be thrilled at the face you see smiling back at you? Picture it. Your skin is softer. It's smoother. Those dark lines are fading away. Can you see that? Let's look at a few products that will make you smile.

EXAMPLE #3: *You're selling candles*

Can you think of a time when you worked so hard to finish a project that you deserved a reward? Are you thinking of a day when you clicked "send" on a work project? How did that feel? Or are you thinking of a day you finally cleaned out that closet? Whatever comes to mind for you, we all know how great we feel when we get things done. *Imagine* yourself at the end of that day stepping into the bathroom to fill the tub for a nice, long soak. *Imagine* surrounding yourself with the warm glow of beautiful candles like these . . .

EXAMPLE #4: *You're selling the hosting opportunity*

Imagine your living room, filled with your friends. Some are milling around the kitchen, others are sitting on the couch. They're having fun catching up. Your living room is so full that you pull a few chairs in from the kitchen. Can you see it? How would that feel? Wouldn't it be fun to fill your house with the laughter of your friends? Did you know that the number one reason hostesses open their homes to a show is that they want to share a fun experience? If you've enjoyed yourself tonight and you've been *imagining* your own living room filled with your friends, let's chat . . .

EXAMPLE #5: *You're selling the hosting opportunity*

Great products, aren't they? Now you can see why people are talking about our company. Can you picture yourself getting dressed to go out, and instead of complaining that you've got nothing to wear, actually having fun choosing which pieces of jewelry to wear? If you've seen a lot of products tonight that make sense for you, picture yourself doing what a lot of people do — opening your home to a party. Think of how it would feel spend a fun evening with your friends and earn a few free products at the same time.

EXAMPLE #6: *You're selling the hosting opportunity*

Imagine yourself at the office coffee pot the morning after your party. Everyone is talking about the amazing appetizers you served the night before. *Imagine* — they're smiling as they share how much fun they had meeting your friends and family. How do you feel knowing that you were the one to make that happen? Let's think about how to make your party so much fun that they're still talking about it weeks later.

EXAMPLE #7: *You're sharing a business opportunity*

You've told me how much you love our products. *Imagine* what it would be like to have products like these in your hands all the time. What do you think you would enjoy most about that? Did you know that as a Consultant you can earn many of our products for free — and, when new products are released, our Consultants are the first to experience them? If you can see yourself turning your love of these products into a fun part-time business, let's take a few moments later to chat . . .

EXAMPLE #8: *You're sharing a business opportunity*

Can you *imagine* how it would feel to have an extra $500 every month? What would you do with those dollars? Put them toward a car payment? Set up a college savings fund? Pay for those "extras" you've always wanted but felt like you couldn't afford? Starting a business like this isn't always about needing the money ... a lot of times, it's opening new possibilities and taking pressure off the monthly budget. I'd love to chat for a few minutes to show you how this business can make a real difference in your life.

EXAMPLE #9: *You're sharing a business opportunity*

Imagine waking up each day with a smile on your face because you're actually looking forward to going to work. How would that feel? Invigorating? Well, I have to say, that's really how I feel about being in this business. OK, I love my time at home with my family — and I also love this: when I go to work, I get to spend time with fun people like you. *Picture yourself* having fun, meeting great people like all of you. Let's talk about how this business could bring you exactly what you're looking for.

RECAP

Imagine helps you tell stories as you create word pictures. When you are aiming to make an emotional connection in a sales conversation, this one word — *Imagine* — is among your most powerful. It helps you guide the customer over the struggle of decision-making, into the joy of owning and enjoying what you have to offer.

Though the story-telling approach takes extra time, the result is a customer who can picture herself with your products. Sales increase when you show how your products are solutions to problems. Business results are stronger when you help customers see how what you offer is a great match for what they want and need.

Imagine is soft. It's effective. And it's best when it's used only a few times during a sales presentation. It's like a highly flavorful spice — most effective when used sparingly. Choose the products in your collection that have the most compelling stories. Plan your sales presentation by carefully placing the *Imagine* approach where it will create the most impact, illuminating the life-enhancing benefits of what you offer.

My words can inspire customers …
…to envision and dream.

Imagine . . .
WORKS WELL WHEN:

- You're selling a product that, on the surface, seems to be ordinary.

- The product you are selling lends itself perfectly to an emotional heart story.

- You want a way to transport your customer from where she is to the exact place where she will enjoy the benefits of your products.

- You're selling an upper-bracket product. Often, the higher the price, the greater the need for buyers to imagine themselves with your product.

- You want your guests to think not just about the tangible benefits of hosting a party, you also want them to connect with the emotional benefits.

QUESTIONS FOR REFLECTION

- Can I remember a personal shopping experience when I imagined? How did my feelings influence my buying decisions?

- As I think about a favorite product, what do I want people to picture themselves doing with that product in their hands? What do I want them to imagine themselves feeling? What will I say in my next selling conversation to paint that picture?

- Which three products in my collection stand out as ideal for the Imagine technique?

- What do customers typically imagine when they think about hosting? What do I want them to imagine? How will I shift what I say to create more inspiring visual pictures?

- What do I want a new team member to picture when she thinks about starting a business? How will I bring the Imagine approach into my recruiting conversations?

SOMETIMES, WHEN YOU'RE SELLING ...

... as your customer listens to your words, she might think to herself

So, what?

You can show how your product
is relevant to her life.

Let's look at a story.

CHAPTER | 6

So, What

Make what you say compelling and relevant.

I graduated in the half of my high school class that made the upper half possible. It's not that I didn't enjoy learning. When it was relevant, it was great fun to learn.

One morning, my American History teacher came into the class and burst into song. He paraded around the front of the room belting out an off-key version of *Swing Low, Sweet Chariot.* This painful performance went on for five minutes before I boldly raised my hand. I asked the question I thought everyone was thinking, *Mr. L, will you please tell us the relevance of all of this?*

Later that morning, defending my actions in the principal's office, I pointed out that it was a teacher's job to make learning relevant. *This teacher did not connect the dots between his song and the lesson we were supposed to learn*, I said. I shared my observation that this was one (and by the way, highly embarrassing) musical performance which did not enhance my learning experience. The Dean of Students commented that my memory of what I said to Mr. L might be distorted.

There's a bit of irony in the fact that I am married to a fifth grade teacher who loves to teach American History. I've learned more about American History as his wife than I ever did as a student. Why? My husband is a master at making history interesting. When I see him working on a lesson which involves a lot of details, he builds in elements of interaction to engage the students. The two words he uses most often are *so, what?* For example, he doesn't simply tell his students about the U.S. Constitution. He recites some of the rights and privileges, then asks them, *So, what does this mean to you? What benefits do you get from these provisions?* He leads students to think about why a lesson matters. He guides them to see history from more than one point of view. He tells stories to make lessons expand well beyond the memorization of facts. Working with antsy fifth graders all day, he has to make his lessons compelling and relevant.

As sales professionals, we face the same challenges that classroom teachers face: we must make our messages compelling and relevant. We have limited time to say what we want to say. Customers get antsy if our messages do not quickly take hold in their hearts and minds. Engage your customers. Help them know why what you're saying matters to them. Keep them on the edges of their chairs, waiting to hear what you will say next. Find words to make your facts interesting. Let's look at two words which can start your story (don't worry, they aren't song and dance). To make each fact more compelling, remember these two words: so, what.

CONCEPT OVERVIEW

Do you appreciate when someone makes an idea meaningful to you, the listener? Have you ever caught yourself over-describing a favorite product, going on and on about its features? Sometimes it's hard to stop yourself once you get on a roll.

So, what invites you to take a deep breath and build a bridge from hard features to soft benefits. The words move you from talking about what something is . . . to what makes it matter. *So, what* helps you transition from speaking to the head to connecting with the heart. Let's look at *So, what* in two ways.

Conversations with yourself. If you overhear yourself doing too much informing and not enough inspiring, invite your inner sales coach to tap you on the shoulder and ask . . . *So, what?* Pause, and rethink what you're saying to make a stronger connection with your customers, their wants, and their needs.

Conversations with customers. As you say the words *So, what* out loud, you will signal the customer that you're about to make your message more relevant. You're about to make your product more compelling. You're about to connect with what matters.

YOU CAN SAY . . .

- *So, what* this means to you is . . .
- *So, what* you will start to feel is . . .
- *So, what* you will discover . . .

Let's look at some examples of this concept in action.

EXAMPLES

EXAMPLE #1: *You're selling health and fitness products*
Our company prides itself on infusing each product with all-natural, high-nutritional impact ingredients. *So, what* you will discover is that now it is easier than ever to transform your health. For example, let's look at this product . . .

EXAMPLE #2: *You're selling kitchen tools*
This is our most popular cookbook. Take a look! Every page includes a beautiful color photograph. *So, what* that means to you is that you can see what it is supposed to look like before you start. And oh, by the way, there are 52 meal plans here. *So, what* you will hear yourself saying every day is *I was so smart to treat myself to this cookbook!*

EXAMPLE #3: *You're selling jewelry*
This collection brings you this season's trendiest colors. *So, what* you can expect is that these pieces will match all of the new fashions out there. And, if you are someone who is looking for an easy way to add a few of the hottest colors to your wardrobe, these pieces will update your look. *So, what* you'll find is you can walk out the door feeling confident and just a little trendy!

EXAMPLE #4: *You're selling the opportunity to host*

This was fun tonight, wasn't it? Our home show presentation lasts about thirty minutes. *So, what* you will find when you host is that you have plenty of time to socialize with your friends and family, as you did tonight. You might want to look at this month's hostess incentive. It's been so popular that I opened up a few more dates.

EXAMPLE #5: *You're selling the opportunity to host*

Our hostesses earn free and discounted products. *So, what* you will discover is that having a party is not only a fun way to get people together, you get to feel the fun of a shopping spree at the end. *So, what* that might mean for you is that bag you really want, but can't seem to justify ordering tonight, well — it could be yours just for opening your home to the fun of a party.

EXAMPLE #6: *You're selling the opportunity to host*

Our parties include a taste-testing experience where everyone gets to sample some of our most popular products. Wouldn't it be fun to have your friends together in your home, nibbling on some amazing appetizers and desserts? We provide the samples and I help you get everything ready. *So, what* this means to you is that the experience is easy, it's fun, and your friends will be talking about you for weeks to come!

EXAMPLE #7: *You're selling a business opportunity*

Our company has been in business for fifteen years. *So, what* that means is that you can feel confident coming into the business, knowing that the wrinkles have been worked out. Best of all, you get to learn from people who have been where you want to go. I love working with people like you. How are you feeling about ordering your business kit so you can jump in and give it a try?

EXAMPLE #8: *You're selling a business opportunity*

Our company is only in its second year of business. *So, what* that means to you is that you get to feel the excitement of being part of our company's beginning. You get to introduce our products and our mission. How would you feel to be part of something new and exciting like this?

EXAMPLE #9: *You're selling a business opportunity*

Our Consultants set their own hours. *So, what* that means to me is that I don't have to sacrifice my life — my business complements my life. I can be there for the third grade play if I want to be, and I can even be the room mother if I want to be. That's my life – what about yours? *So, what* would a flexible schedule mean to you?

RECAP

It's up to you, the sales professional, to balance a sales conversation with a blend of information and inspiration. It's easy to get caught up in talking about features. While a particular product may be known for its characteristics, you can make that product more compelling by going beyond facts and bringing feelings into what you say.

Show your customers what will make your products important in their lives. Take your selling conversations from what a product is to why it will matter to them. Use these two simple words: *So, what* — to make each feature more relevant to your customer's life.

So, what is also about self-talk. Train yourself to think about what you say, thinking *So, what makes this important to the person I'm talking with?* You can pivot when you catch yourself talking too much. Pause. Rethink your approach. Infuse your words with life-enhancing benefits that make your products and services simply irresistible.

Selling is more than telling.

So, what ...
WORKS WELL WHEN:

- You're selling a product that is not easily understood. Some products call for demonstration. *So, what* helps you to do more than show and tell — it invites you to sell.

- You're selling a technical product that needs extensive explanation. *So, what* helps you make a detailed feature come to life.

- You've been talking a lot, and you can tell that you are losing your audience.

- You are explaining your opportunity to a recruiting prospect, and you want to shift the focus from what you have to offer to what she's looking for.

QUESTIONS FOR REFLECTION

- What challenges are my customers facing in their everyday lives? What makes my products a relevant solution?

- Which of my products is the most complicated to explain? What are the most important facts about that product? How can I adjust my sales presentation to make those facts more compelling?

- What is it about my favorite product that makes it my favorite? If my mind went to a fact, feature, or characteristic, how can I use *So, what* to get to the heart of its life-enhancing benefits?

- Which element of my company's host rewards program is most exciting to my hosts? How can I move from telling about that feature, to selling that feature, when I'm talking with a potential host?

- What do prospective team members need to know about our company's start-up plan? How can I make the "need-to-know" information inspiring and relevant to their lives?

SOMETIMES, WHEN
YOU'RE SELLING . . .
. . . something's getting in the way.

"You may be thinking . . ."
Opens the door to discuss concerns.

Let's look at a story.

CHAPTER | 7

You May Be Thinking

Invite concerns that limit the view of possibilities.

I smiled as I pulled into my hostess's driveway. I had a feeling that this was going to be a great show.

As I stepped out of the car, I was enthusiastically greeted by a sandy-colored dog. Clearly, this dog was more excited to meet me than I was to meet him. I've never had a dog, and I think they sense my lack of dog-handling expertise. When dogs encounter me, they naturally increase their level of sniffing, licking, and overall friendliness. They know I just won't know what to do.

My hostess' sister greeted me at the door. For each of my three trips back and forth to the car, my hyperactive furry friend was at my side every step of the way. As I set up my display in the family room, Jane, my hostess, stopped in to say hello before walking to the kitchen to start a pot of coffee. I finished arranging my display with the dog at my side. I got to thinking that Jane was more abrupt than I had remembered. Maybe she'd had a bad day.

I stepped into the kitchen to start cooking appetizers with

Jane, accompanied by my four-legged friend. As Jane and I chatted, I noticed that she was clearly distracted and unhappy about something. I asked, *Jane, is everything okay?* She lifted a small block of cream cheese from the fridge, and slammed it on the counter. I wondered, *What is going on here?* Something was definitely keeping her from having fun.

Looking at me with a puzzled expression, she said, *Sue, I have a question.* She went on to ask, *Do you always bring your dog to your shows?* I was a bit puzzled, and said, *I don't have a dog!* She replied. *Then, whose dog is this?* I thought about that quickly before responding, *I don't know. When he greeted me at my car, I just assumed he was yours.*

Jane was stuck on the thought that I had brought my dog along to her home. Imagine that! This thought kept her from thinking about anything else. When I sensed there was something in the way, I finally just asked if everything was okay so we could move forward.

When you are selling, your customers often have thoughts in their way, too. They have concerns which keep them from seeing possibilities. You can take the lead by asking questions. Make it possible for your customers to explore new and different possibilities.

By the way, Jane and I later discovered a moving van down the street. The new family was so busy that they lost sight of their dog. While out looking for new friends, he found me.

CONCEPT OVERVIEW

Have you ever encountered a situation where someone held on to an idea so tightly that she couldn't see different possibilities? As you learn your products, you learn your customers' most common hesitations. As we know, hesitations can block the customer's view of what is possible.

When a customer raises a hesitation during a group selling presentation, a thought that concerns only one person can have a negative impact on the thinking of everyone. *You may be thinking* opens the door to proactively address common concerns. You can head off potentially negative thoughts by bringing them up before anyone else does.

Whether you're in a one-on-one selling situation or selling to a group, at times you may need a tool to redirect thought. This way of *saying it softly* will keep you from having to feel defensive as you respond to a concern. *You may be thinking* provides a graceful way to get ahead of concerns, turning could-be negatives into positive thoughts.

YOU CAN SAY . . .

- *"You may be thinking . . ."*
- "You may have noticed . . ."
- "You may be wondering . . ."

Let's look at some examples of this concept in action . . .

EXAMPLES

EXAMPLE #1: *You're selling home décor*
You may be thinking . . . *these bright bold colors would never match my color scheme.* A lot of people feel that way when they first see this collection. What they find is that a splash of vivid color is invigorating. These tones are not intended to match, they are meant to complement your existing color scheme, and to inspire a feeling of boldness. Who already owns a piece from this collection?

EXAMPLE #2: *You're selling scrapbooking products*
You may be thinking . . . *how much time will it take to create a finished digital album like this one?* A lot of people wonder about that. Some say it takes as little as an evening—others say it can take as much as a weekend. It's up to you. Either way, you'll feel great when you're done. You can make yours as simple or complex as you feel like making it! What people love is that you do the layout just once, and then you can make as many copies as you want with no extra time.

EXAMPLE #3: *You're selling home organization products*
You may be thinking . . . *products like these are for people who are already organized, not someone like me!* I felt that way when I first saw them, too, and what I've discovered is that these products have made it easy to organize my life, one corner at a time. They make me feel I'm managing my life instead of letting it manage me.

EXAMPLE # 4: *You're selling the opportunity to host*

You may be thinking . . . *that this is not a good time to consider having a party, this time of year is just too busy with getting ready for the holidays.* You're right — this is a busy time for everyone, and that's the very reason people appreciate being invited to stop and take a break and enjoy a fun time with friends. How would you feel to have your friends thanking you for the invitation to relax and enjoy a glass of wine?

EXAMPLE # 5: *You're selling the opportunity to host*

You may be thinking . . . *that if you were to have a party, you'd have to find a bunch of people who already enjoy making hand-made cards.* What hostesses find about having a party like this is that everyone has fun, and everyone learns a thing or two about how easy it is to be creative. You may be surprised, actually. Sometimes the people you think would never have an interest are the ones who have the most fun!

EXAMPLE #6: *You're selling the opportunity to host*

You may be thinking . . . *your friends live crazy-busy lives, and you feel like it might be hard to get them together.* I understand! If you're like most people, you've run into more than one friend and said "let's get together sometime!" — and then life got in the way. Sometimes all of us need a reason to stop and connect with the people we enjoy. You can be the one to give your friends a reason to slow down and enjoy time together.

EXAMPLE # 7: *You're selling a business opportunity*

You may be thinking *that in order to make room for a business like this, you'd have to make significant changes to your life.* You'd be surprised. While you can work as much or as little as you like, our average Consultant does about a show a week. At that pace, you feel like you're in business but it doesn't feel overwhelming. How could you see something like this fitting into your life?

EXAMPLE # 8: *You're selling a business opportunity*

You may be wondering *how you would learn what you need to know about our products.* That's the fun part. Our Business Starter Kit comes with eighteen products, and easy-to-follow information that helps you know what will be most important to your friends and family. You already love our products. That's why you'll feel confident selling them.

EXAMPLE # 9: *You're selling a business opportunity*

Are you thinking that *. . . to get involved with a business like this, you have to be someone who likes selling?* I was surprised when I realized that what I really do is help people have something they love … chocolate … in their lives more often! Think about how excited you were to experience this tonight. You may enjoy doing something like this more than you imagined!

RECAP

A hesitation can get stuck in a customer's mind, and keep her from seeing the possibilities a product can hold for herself, her family, and for her life. Think about hesitations as boulders on your customer's path. What you do as a sales professional is help her move a boulder out of the way so she can keep moving forward.

Show confidence, preparedness, and an openness to talk about all dimensions of a product. When you proactively raise common hesitations before customers do, you shine a light on the positives of the product. Help your customers feel trust in you, and trust in the fact that you know what may be getting in their way.

You may be thinking gives you a way to confidently put it all out on the table, without hiding anything. This helps your customer let go of thoughts which limit her view, and helps her to think about possibilities.

It's up to me …
to get ahead of hesitations.

You may be thinking . . .
WORKS WELL WHEN:

- You're selling a product with a bold feature, such as a bright color, large size, or dramatic style.

- People tend to think your product is just for a certain kind of person.

- There is a perception that using your product will take a lot of time.

- Your product is considered to be expensive.

- Your product appears, on the surface, to be just like others they've seen.

- You want to bring a recruiting prospect's hesitations out in the open.

QUESTIONS FOR REFLECTION

- How do I feel when I sense a customer's objection?

- What general concerns do I hear most often in conversations about my products?

- What will I do to get ahead of those concerns?

- What product objections do I hear frequently? What will I say to turn would-be negatives into positive thoughts?

- What hesitations do I hear most often about hosting? How will I boldly anticipate their concerns?

- What gets people stuck when it comes to thinking about the business? How will I adjust my recruiting approach?

SOMETIMES, WHEN
YOU'RE SELLING . . .

*. . . your customers' choices aren't
tough at all.*

Your toughest choice

shifts thinking
from whether to buy
to which to buy.

Let's look at a story.

CHAPTER 8

Your Toughest Choice

Lead your customer to consider choices.

Each spring, as Girl Scout Cookie season gets underway, I look forward to the ring of the doorbell. There's something quite endearing about the bright smile of an enthusiastic Girl Scout standing at the door ready to test her selling skills. I am an easy mark. When I peer through the window and see a Girl Scout sash, I know that my toughest choice won't be *if* to buy, it will be *what* to buy.

My son overheard my conversation with the second cookie seller of the day. He paid close attention as the young lady stumbled through her rehearsed sales talk. He listened carefully as I asked questions. First, I asked her to share what she enjoys most about being a Girl Scout. Then I asked, *So, how are your cookie sales going so far? How close are you to reaching your goal?* After hearing about her goals and progress, I did what any sales trainer would do: I encouraged her to keep going. *You're doing great. Keep at it! You're enthusiastic and you can do this.* And then my inner sales trainer kicked in, and I said something like this: *I could use your help making some tough choices today. Which type of cookie is your favorite?* Inviting her to describe the cookie, I asked, *So, what do you think makes that cookie so special?*

As this young lady walked away, my son asked, *Mom, seriously. What was that all about? You know you're going to buy cookies. Why do you make those girls work so hard for the sale? Aren't you being a little mean?* I thought about it before answering. *I want the experience of selling cookies to do something for them. I want them to leave our house knowing they really earned the sale.*

You earn your sales, in part, by helping customers over the pain of yes or no decisions. Customers stop thinking about *whether* to buy as soon as they start thinking about *which* to buy. Which products do you sell that lend themselves perfectly to a discussion of choices?

By the way, when I'm buying Girl Scout cookies, the choices are not difficult. I've never met a Girl Scout cookie I didn't like. **My toughest choice** is whether to buy two boxes or three.

When we order more cookies than any one household should, we send packages overseas. I like to say *thanks* to the men and women who serve our country, and this allows me to think of my purchase as a win/win/win. My cookie purchase becomes a win for the seller who came to the door. It's a win for the soldiers who get to enjoy the cookies. And it's a win for me, as I get to fulfill my inner need to mentor budding entrepreneurs and show appreciation to others. Oh, and is there such a thing as too many Thin Mints?

CONCEPT OVERVIEW

It is exciting to discover words and phrases that help you place your products in the best possible light. ***Your toughest choice*** works perfectly when you're presenting your customer with a variety of options.

Your toughest choice leads the customer to stop thinking about whether to buy, and start thinking about which to buy. It's not an assumptive technique meant to manipulate. It's a playful, yet very strategic, approach. ***Your toughest choice*** uses the word tough, but this approach works best when there's nothing tough about the choices at all. They're all good.

Some words and phrases fit best as you begin talking about a product. However, ***Your toughest choice*** works best near the end of what you say. You'll be most effective when you start by establishing interest in the base product, without bringing choice into your discussion. Once you've created excitement for the base product, you can use this approach to introduce the element of choice.

YOU CAN SAY . . .

- ***Your toughest choice . . .***

- Which would be better, this one or that one?

- ***The toughest choice*** you'll have to make . . .

Let's look at some examples of this concept in action.

EXAMPLES

EXAMPLE #1: *You're selling candles*
Don't you love the size of this decorative Hurricane? What people tell me they like best about this is that it works in a number of settings. This beautiful candle holder even looks great at an outside party — the flame stays deep inside, protected even on a windy night. Where can you picture this in your home? *Your toughest choice* will be whether to fill your Hurricane with a Fresh Citrus candle or our new Essence of Herbs fragrance.

EXAMPLE #2: *You're selling jewelry*
This necklace is one of our most popular designs. I think the reason people love it so much is that black looks great with everything. Doesn't it? Does this piece look like something you'd enjoy? *Your toughest choice* will be to decide on the 18-inch princess length, or the longer 22-inch matinee length.

EXAMPLE #3: *You're selling garden tools*
We're so confident in the quality of our gardening tools, we back them with a year's guarantee. Sturdy handles like these mean that your hands won't have to do all of the work. *Your toughest choice* will be whether to go with our basic package of these three tools . . . or, to do what a lot of people do . . . and treat your hands to our inclusive package that brings you five of our most popular gardening tools.

EXAMPLE #4: *You're selling the opportunity to host*

I know that Susan has loved having all of you here tonight. I hope you've had fun, too. If you are thinking about bringing your friends together, think of what you'd enjoy most about an experience like this. This is really an easy party to put together. As you think about hosting, ***the toughest choice*** you'll need to make is whether you want to host an evening party, as Susan has done, or do what a lot of people do, and host a Saturday morning party. Think about it, you'd put on a pot of coffee, and . . .

EXAMPLE #5: *You're selling the opportunity to host*

Did you know that the #1 reason hostesses have a party is to share a fun experience with their friends? If that's something you're thinking about, I'd love to tell you more. At our company, we make every day a good day for hostesses to get together for a party. Hostesses look forward to not only the fun — but also some pretty exciting thank-you gifts. ***Your toughest choice*** will be whether to host a party next month, or jump on the opportunity to get this item for free by hosting a party this month.

EXAMPLE #6: *You're selling the opportunity to host*

You know, part of what makes a party really fun is that it's different depending on who's there. I like to focus the experience on the needs of the guests. What do you think would be a better fit for you — a party experience where we really dive into our XYZ collection, or, do you think your friends would prefer to explore time-saving ideas for the upcoming season?

EXAMPLE #7: *You're selling a business opportunity*

I can see that you're excited to get started. This is going to be fun for you — and you're going to find that working the business is easier than you might think. ***Your toughest choice,*** really, is to decide whether you want to begin with our Basic Starter Kit, or do what a lot of people do and order our Deluxe Starter Kit.

EXAMPLE #8: *You're selling a business opportunity*

What's great about a business like this is that you get to make the decisions about how much you work, when you work, and even how much you earn. How would that feel? **Your toughest choice** will be to decide whether to save your earnings for a vacation or treat yourself to something special! As you think about getting started, what gets you most excited?

EXAMPLE #9: *You're selling a business opportunity*

I know you haven't decided yet whether you want to give the business a try. I'm wondering, though, ***which would be better for you?*** Would you see yourself doing one party a week, which is just four out of thirty nights a month? Or, do you see yourself doing two parties a week? I'm wondering, would it help your decision if we compared the potential earning picture for you, looking at one and two parties a week?

RECAP

As a sales professional, you're in the business of matching a person's needs and wants with the products you have to offer. Sometimes your product line offers a variety of choices that all lead to the same outcome. More than anything, you present choices to match personal preferences.

There is an art to introducing the element of choice. You don't want to confuse your customer. Instead, you want to inspire swift decision-making. As you bring **Your toughest choice** into your sales vocabulary, consider the strategy behind the words:

- Effective selling is about establishing interest in the base product first. Help your customer realize that no matter which selection she makes, she'll get to the underlying benefits you've shared with her.

- Most people find it more difficult to decide *if* to take action than to decide *which type* of action to take. You can help a customer skip the agony of making a yes/no decision — by shifting her to think about her options.

The choices you're talking about are anything but tough choices!

Your toughest choice . . .
WORKS WELL WHEN:

- Your product is offered in a variety of colors, flavors, fragrances, or styles.

- Your product is offered in both a single-pack and a multiple-pack form.

- Your product is offered in a variety of sizes, all of which meet the same basic needs.

- Your business enrollment program offers a number of choices.

Note: *Your toughest choice* is not an ideal approach when you are presenting something which actually is a tough choice.

QUESTIONS FOR REFLECTION

- Which products in my collection provide the customer with a variety of options?

- As I think about products that offer choices, what are the core benefits that make a difference regardless of the customer's selection?

- How am I thinking differently about the way I sell a product with options?

- What choices do prospective hosts make as they consider opening their home to a party? How can I be more effective in discussing those choices?

- What decisions does a prospective team member make at the time she decides to start a business? How can I simplify the choices?

SOMETIMES, WHEN
YOU'RE SELLING . . .
. . . *you would love to bring
satisfied customers along.*

What people tell me

helps you share one customer's
experience with another.

Let's look at a story.

CHAPTER | 9

What people tell me

Share the inspiration and wisdom of past customers.

When income increases by small amounts each month, we don't always realize that the raises are becoming significant. Like a baby growing into a toddler, sometimes we fail to notice growth. When I realized that my part-time venture was generating income that my family had come to depend on, I knew it was time to buy life insurance.

I was invited to serve as a field representative on my company's long-range planning committee. While making my travel arrangements, I got to thinking: *I am investing a couple of days in the company's long-term planning; what about my own long-term planning?* Before children, such things as life insurance were part of my employee benefit package at my corporate job. *What would life be like for my husband and children if anything happened to me?*

After I dropped the boys at kindergarten, I thought about it. What was I waiting for? The idea of buying my own life insurance made me feel proud. Almost excited. Definitely grown-up and quite accomplished. It seemed like a symbolic step that acknowledged my business was now real. I took a common 1987 approach to gather information. Opening the Yellow Pages to "I" for Insurance, my first call was to Gary. He did what good insurance agents do: he asked questions.

He helped me realize what I was really looking for: the *feeling* of knowing that my family's needs would be met if anything happened to me. Gary built trust with me before probing about our family's finances. I asked for his help as I tried to figure out what size policy to buy.

It was clear that Gary had sold plenty of insurance policies, and he had experience helping people make decisions like these. I told him I didn't know where to begin to decide how much insurance to buy. Gary could have pulled out an agreement and said *I think this is what you should buy.* Instead, he took a soft-selling approach. He said, **what people tell me** *gives them the most comfort is to provide for the mortgage and some coverage of income.* He suggested I add coverage for the value of child care, as my husband would need to pay for that so he could go to work every day. He took out a calculator and we decided on an amount. That day, I purchased my first, modest, life insurance policy.

What people tell me led me to feel like I was somehow connected with Gary's other clients. At the same time, Gary's approach built his own credibility. I was alone, buying my first life insurance policy, but I felt like others were standing at my side helping me make my decision. I never asked Gary how many other clients felt proud and excited about buying life insurance. I just know I was.

CONCEPT OVERVIEW

In a sense, this selling approach invites you to bring every one of your delighted customers along to each selling opportunity. Let's look at it this way: You're the soloist, singing the main tune. Your back-up chorus adds a range of tones to support your voice.

Third party opinions have the potential to create a powerful, yet soft, effect. **What people tell me** opens your presentation and invites customers to draw on the experiences of others as they form their own views. When you intentionally bring your chorus of happy customers with you, you shed a different light on the soft benefits of your products and services. This phrase helps you be with just one potential client and feel like you're in a room filled with all of your past clients singing your praises.

Just as Gary shared the wisdom of past customers with me, you can share the experiences of your past customers with current customers. Share their inspiration. Share their satisfaction. Help today's customers know how yesterday's customers felt using and enjoying your products.

YOU CAN SAY . . .

- Last week, a client told me how much . . .

- **What people tell me** they love most about this . . .

- **What people tell me** they discover when they use this is . . .

Let's look at some examples of this concept in action.

EXAMPLES

EXAMPLE #1: *You're selling personalized gifts*

What people tell me about this bag as a wedding or shower gift is how fun it is to create something that is truly one-of-a-kind. One of my customers created a picnic tote by filling it with a plaid blanket, plates, and bottle of wine. Another client told me that she filled it with seasonal plates and napkins, a bottle of champagne, and a card wishing the couple a year of celebrating the seasons together. How would you feel to see the couple's names, or monogram, on the front, right here . . .

EXAMPLE #2: *You're selling educational books*

What people tell me they appreciate most are not the messages in the books, but the moments that the books create. Last week, one of my customers told me how it felt when her three-year-old granddaughter came running in the front door saying *Grandma, will you read me a story?* What would that feel like for you?

EXAMPLE #3: *You're selling skin care*

What people tell me is that they love the compliments they receive as people notice their younger-looking skin. The other day, a client called to share an experience. She was at a business appointment, and one of her associates pulled her aside to ask how difficult it was to recover from her plastic surgery. My client didn't know what to say. Her results from using our products were so noticeable that it looked like she'd had surgery. How would that make you feel?

EXAMPLE #4: *You're selling the opportunity to host*

What hostesses tell me they appreciate most about hosting a show is that they enjoy connecting with people they haven't seen for a long time. If you're like most people, life presents chances to see your family members and some of your friends. How often, though, do you see friends from your old neighborhood, former co-workers, or people whose paths don't cross yours as often as they once did? How would it feel to slow down and catch up for awhile?

EXAMPLE #5: *You're selling the opportunity to host*

What people often tell me is that the main reason they decide to host a party is because it's fun. They have a good time — and they want to share a good time with friends and neighbors. When the party is over, *people tell me* that they're glad they hosted for so many reasons. More than once, I've had a hostess tell me that seeing all of the benefits earned by hosting feels a lot like Christmas morning, full of exciting surprises!

EXAMPLE #6: *You're selling the value of reminder calls*

. . . I understand. The idea of making reminder calls does seem, on the surface, like an extra step. You feel like you don't want to push your friends, yet think about this. *What people tell me* is that it's easier to make the calls than they expected. Most hostesses find that they can make a quick call to everyone on the list in less than an hour. What I hear most often is that with people being so busy, it's not uncommon for half of them to arrive at the party saying *thank you for that reminder call, I would have forgotten about the date!* Wouldn't that make you feel good?

EXAMPLE #7: *You're selling a business opportunity*

You can probably tell that I have a lot of fun doing this business — that's because it allows me to connect with people like you. What you might not know is I get to work with women who have a great time together. Whether I'm chatting with a team member who started so she could break the monotony of her full-time job, or I'm visiting with a retired schoolteacher who was looking for a way to stay involved with people, I seem to hear the same thing. **What I hear most often** is that the business is more fun than they ever expected it to be. What about you? What would you enjoy the most about being involved?

EXAMPLE #8: *You're selling a business opportunity*

Our Basic Starter Kit has everything you need to get started. It's really surprising how much you receive for this low startup investment. **What people tell me** is how excited they feel when they see so many product samples in the carton. It's so fun to experience the products.

EXAMPLE #9: *You're helping a new team member start*

It's been a few years since I started my business. I haven't forgotten, though, how it felt to make my first phone calls. When I'm talking with new team members, **what people tell me** is that this first page in our Startup Guide really helps to build confidence to book those first dates. Let's look, here, at how it guides you to start off strong.

RECAP

What people tell me is more than a set of words. It's a concept that broadens the way you look at your role as a sales professional. Part of what you do in selling is share ideas gleaned through your own experiences with products. And sometimes sharing someone else's ideas, through a fresh point of view, has more impact than sharing your own. Experienced sellers know that bringing a past client's experience to a current client adds impact and increases your sales effectiveness.

You're a facilitator. You bring people together. The diverse voices of your most satisfied customers will help you sing the praises of your company, your products, and your services. You are ***selling it softly***. Invite your back-up chorus to lend a hand as you create your own story of success.

Connect one person's positive experience
with another person's potential experience.

What people tell me ...
WORKS WELL WHEN:

- You're selling a product that is not one of your personal favorites. Perhaps this item does not suit your personal taste. ***What people tell me*** allows you to maintain your authenticity, sharing the insights and experiences of others who have a passion for the product.

- You are selling a product that you have not yet personally experienced.

- You are selling a top-selling item that your customers commonly boast about.

- You want to tell a story from someone else's point of view.

- It's been a long time since you started your business, and you want to help a business prospect connect with how it feels to get started.

QUESTIONS FOR REFLECTION

- What's the strongest satisfied client testimonial I have ever received? How can I bring that client's experience into my selling and sponsoring conversations?

- Which products do people rave about most often? What have I heard from past customers that could influence the thinking of a prospective customer?

- What do I hear most often from my hosts when the party is over? What do they say on the day the order arrives? How can I capture their positive experiences and share them with my prospective hosts?

- What have I learned from my fellow team members? How can I bring their product ideas and experiences into my selling and sponsoring conversations?

- Who do I know in the business with an experience quite different from mine? Who is at a very different stage of life from mine and enjoying different aspects of the career experience? How can I capture some of their positive insights and bring them into my sponsoring conversations?

SOMETIMES, WHEN
YOU'RE SELLING ...
... *you help people see things
differently.*

Have you thought about

invites people to stretch their thinking.

Let's look at a story.

CHAPTER | **10**

Have you thought about

Open your customer's mind to see things differently.

Of all my corporate work at Crayola®, I most enjoyed my time with the field. Each meeting I had with a Consultant or Leader allowed me to reconnect with the heart of the business. It was important that I showed respect for all that they were doing to grow the business, and at the same time, I liked to stretch their thinking about the business.

To gain insight about customer perceptions of our products and home party experience, I observed home parties in various parts of the country. Guests and hostesses poured out their heartfelt stories of past experiences with the brand. They shared how it felt as a child to open their first box of crayons, or how it felt to introduce Crayola® products to their children and grandchildren. All our Consultants had to do was say the brand name, and customers made an immediate emotional connection with their childhood experiences. I realized that we had a marketing challenge: in this new party-plan division, just who was our customer?

Direct selling success calls for the head and the heart to work together. The emotional reaction to Crayola® products was clear. It was the thought process that needed some work. Consumer thinking centered on the company's existing products, and existing target audience: children. I was familiar with one of the realities of the party plan model, that parties are most successful when they are well-attended. I felt that prospective hostesses should invite non-moms, as well as moms. The thinking was that a more generationally-diverse audience would result in a more measurably-successful and satisfying party.

We spent a lot of time working on positioning, maintaining respect for the established brand while expanding the party-plan customer's thinking to see new possibilities. Our catalog suggested that we offered *products inspiring kids of all ages to experience and share the joy of creativity.* It took work — a lot of work — to open a customer's mind to see things differently. Consultants worked hard to help hostesses and guests see that creative experiences could include everyone, asking **have you thought about** *how it would feel to take a break from your busy life and discover your own creative spirit?*

I discovered that when memories and feelings are deeply rooted in our minds and hearts, change is not easy. I also learned that when you invite people to explore new possibilities, you stretch their thinking, and that is a worthwhile effort. We never know where an idea can take someone if we keep it to ourselves. Wouldn't you agree, life is far more colorful when we inspire each other to think differently?

CONCEPT OVERVIEW

When you're selling, at times you might have a message that stretches your customer's thinking. **Have you thought about** gives you a soft way to invite and suggest. Instead of a direct command telling people what they should be doing, you can gently, suggestively invite someone to think differently, or to learn more about what you have to share.

Have you thought about also allows you to measure interest without using the word *interested*. People don't always like to admit that they have an interest, because the word *interested* implies more commitment than many feel is comfortable. Limit your use of the word interested, and replace it with the **have you thought about** phrase.

Compare these two approaches:

- are you interested in hosting a party?

- have **you thought about** hosting a party?

Can you hear the difference?

YOU CAN SAY . . .

- Have you wondered if . . .

- Have you considered looking at . . .

- *Have you thought about . . .*

Let's look at some examples of this concept in action.

EXAMPLES

EXAMPLE #1: *You're selling cosmetics and skincare*
Have you thought at all about how many hours of your week you spend sleeping? I know, maybe not enough! Think about this for a moment — while you are asleep, your skin is busy renewing cells. Until now, you may not have thought about what you can do to make that renewal process work even harder for you. Let's look at how we can give it a little help . . .

EXAMPLE #2: *You're selling gourmet food*
Wouldn't you agree, it's easy to get stuck in a rut? You know what I mean. Making the same things, day after day, week after week? As you've been sampling some of these foods tonight, you may be asking yourself which sauce, which salad dressing, or which mix you'd like to try first. Let me ask you this: ***Have you thought about*** what life would be like to open your pantry every day of the week and be met with a new, fun choice to try? How would that feel — would you be excited to plan meals and cook again? I invite you to open your catalog to the section here where you will see our packages. What people tell me they love most is . . .

EXAMPLE #3: *You're selling stylish, functional bags and totes*
Life just feels simpler when we're organized, doesn't it? ***Have you thought about*** how much time you lose looking for the things you need when you want to go somewhere? How great would it be to have

a few simple totes when you want to get out the door? Like this simple business tote ready to greet you each morning, with a spot for your glasses so they're there when you need them. Or, this travel tote that you can pre-pack with your small-sized toiletries, taking the hassle out of getting ready for a quick weekend getaway. ***Have you thought about*** what life would be like to leave your house feeling organized?

EXAMPLE #4: *You're selling the opportunity to host*
Have you thought about what makes this a great month to have a party? Any time of year can be a good time to get friends together, and here's what makes this month so special …

EXAMPLE #5: *You're selling the opportunity to host*
From time to time, someone tells me they'd like to have a party but they just don't think they have the space. They're picturing the exact number of upholstered seats in their living room, instead of picturing their friends having fun. ***Have you thought about*** how much more fun a party is when the house is so full that people sit everywhere?

EXAMPLE #6: *You're selling the opportunity to host*
You like the idea of a party, but you feel a little uncomfortable inviting friends over to shop in your home. ***Have you thought at all about*** how your friends might feel to get together at your house and experience what we did tonight — a lot of laughter, a few ideas, and a little inspiration?

EXAMPLE #7: *You're selling a business opportunity*

Have you thought about doing what I'm doing? I am having a great time being involved with this company, and I'm thinking that you might enjoy it, too. I'd love to tell you more. Is there a time when we can chat for a few minutes to explore possibilities?

EXAMPLE #8: *You're selling a business opportunity*

A lot of people think that a business like this means you have to be out at night. They think about how tired they feel at the end of the day, and they can't even imagine themselves working evenings. You can do parties when it works for you, whether that's evenings or weekends. Let me ask you this: *Have you thought about* how much energy you would draw from lifting others with your presentation and products?

EXAMPLE #9: *You're selling a business opportunity*

Have you ever noticed how many people buy lottery tickets? It seems like a lot of people today are thinking about what it would be like to have some extra money. *Have you thought about* how it would feel to pay off that bill . . . or to set aside a little bit each month for that special vacation next year? Let's connect for a few minutes later if you like the idea of earning a little extra money each month. We can look at the odds of winning the lottery, compared with the odds of making a real difference in your budget going out just a few nights a month . . .

RECAP

Your catalog shows beautiful pictures of your products, carefully photographed to place each item in the best possible light. Your catalog might include pictures of people as they enjoy using your products, and detailed information about physical features and functional benefits. Yet, even the best catalog can't make the suggestions that you can make when you are ***selling it softly***.

As you share your products, you also share experiences and stories to stretch a customer's thinking about what you're really selling. You stretch them to try things they may never have considered trying.

This phrase will expand your selling vocabulary, inviting customers to explore new ways of thinking about what you have to offer. As a sales professional, it's important that you measure interest throughout the selling process. Softly, you can replace the word "interested" with a question that begins with ***have you thought about***. Not only will this approach expand your customer's thinking, you'll open conversations that explore new possibilities.

We don't know
what we don't know.

Have you thought about . . .
WORKS WELL WHEN:

- You want to make a suggestion without presenting yourself as "preachy."

- Your customer has preconceived thoughts about your company, products, your opportunity, or home party experience. You want to softly challenge her thinking without being confrontational.

- You see possibilities that your customer may have never considered.

- You are aware of common buying patterns, and you want to stretch your customer to think in new ways.

- You're inviting someone to learn more about the business.

QUESTIONS FOR REFLECTION

- What do I know about my products that I wish my customers knew? How can I adjust my sales approach to invite customers to broaden their thinking?

- What suggestions could I make to help customers get more of what they want and need? How can I use the words have you thought about to introduce those suggestions?

- In what circumstances do I find myself inadvertently using the word "interested?"

- In what ways does the word "interested" get in the way of connecting with a prospective team member?

- What could a softer approach do for me and my business?

SOMETIMES, WHEN
YOU'RE SELLING . . .

*. . . all it takes is one detail to move
from
99% thinking about it
to 100% sold.*

Oh, by the way ...

is your way of introducing that detail.

Let's look at a story.

CHAPTER | 11

Oh, by the way

Keep a favorite feature or benefit in your back pocket.

Growing up in the Chicago suburbs, I considered State Fairs to be largely a rural experience. Farmers showcasing livestock did not seem like an entertaining experience to a suburbanite like me. Until we moved to Minnesota, I didn't know what a State Fair could be.

Referred to as "The Great Minnesota Get-Together," the State Fair attracts millions of visitors each year. More than a celebration of agriculture, rides, and entertainment, it is also known for providing a forum for knowledge and new ideas. You can actually watch likenesses of young *Princesses of the Milky Way* being carved out of ninety-pound blocks of butter. Seriously. Oh, and the food at the Minnesota State Fair is amazing.

The exhibit buildings are among my favorites. It's fun to wander through the booths where vendors market an endless variety of home products. Whether they're selling the latest and greatest floor mop, a special device for more effective car-washing, or a must-have piece of kitchen equipment, these vendors offer rich learning experiences for anyone in sales.

Equipped with headset microphones, the sellers begin by gathering a crowd. They shout out to fair-goers, asking easy-to-answer questions which draw them in. They masterfully attract attention. Their fast-talking selling skills, while cheesy, are impressive.

The State Fair selling style has way too much of a "pitch" feel for my taste. That said, watching a State Fair pro in action can be quite educational. So can watching customers as they gather around and listen. You can't help but notice that State Fair sellers have great timing. Just when a customer looks like she's ready to say "no," the salesperson introduces the last, most compelling benefit. The grand finale. The big *ta da*. This last benefit statement typically inspires the customer to move from 99% interested to 100% ready to buy. For example, the seller may announce that his special mop comes with extra attachments for those hard-to-reach places.

One of the showiest products I ever sold was a tool for chopping food. It was fun to talk about this product because customers loved how it made life easier in the kitchen. The State Fair experience taught me to keep one key benefit in my back pocket. Knowing that the feature of easy cleanup created a lot of excitement, especially after a customer had discovered the product's benefits, I learned to say ***oh, by the way**, wait until you see how easy this is to clean!* I'd be met with oohs and aahs as I opened the chopper before their eyes. It wouldn't take long to hear the question, *where can I find this product on the order form?* The vendors at the State Fair would be proud.

CONCEPT OVERVIEW

Here, you put timing on your side. Instead of leading with your most impressive feature or benefit, you pace yourself. Knowing that your customer needs time to process her thoughts and feelings, you intentionally keep a key feature or benefit in your back pocket until the end of your presentation on that product.

You're not trying to manipulate the customer. You're saving that last benefit to delight and surprise your customer to the extent that she feels excited to buy.

Oh, by the way works especially well when you have a piece of factual or logical information that can make your customer feel better about her buying decision. Establish the emotional connection. Then, support her interest in buying with that last little feature, that special offer, or that detail that flips her from just thinking about it … to making the decision.

YOU CAN SAY ...

- *Oh, by the way*, did I tell you …

- I almost forgot! Did I tell you …

- Oh, did I mention …

Let's look at some examples of this concept in action.

EXAMPLES

EXAMPLE #1: *You're selling stationery and paper*

I'm sure you agree, this is no ordinary stationery. When you send a note or letter written on this delicate paper, you're making quite the statement. ***Oh, by the way***, you are going to love the decorative box that comes with this product. Can you see this beautiful box sitting impressively on your desktop?

EXAMPLE #2: *You're selling stylish, functional bags and totes*

Face it, it's hard enough to find the time to get to the gym. You don't want to add another chunk of time to get organized to get to the gym! People love this bag for so many uses. Just last week I was with some women who use this exclusively as their go-to-gym bag. They keep it pre-packed so they take away every excuse and get themselves out the door at the snap of their fingers. It comes in a number of fun colors — they're all fun and stylish. And ***oh, by the way*** — on this side, there's a pocket for your water bottle, and here, this zippered pouch is a great place to store your ear buds . . .

EXAMPLE #3: *You're selling home cleaning products*

You're looking at one of our most popular fragrances. It's refreshing, isn't it? ***Did I mention that*** all of the ingredients here are completely natural and environmentally friendly?

EXAMPLE #4: *You're selling the opportunity to host*

If you've been thinking that you might want to open your home to the fun of a show, let's find a second to chat about what our host program is all about (describe benefits). Hostesses love what they earn. Most of all, they love bringing friends together the way Holly has tonight. *Oh, by the way*, our new collection kicks off on the first of next month. What that means to you is that I'll have new things to share at your party, things that will get your friends thinking about the fun of the upcoming season.

EXAMPLE #5: *You're selling the opportunity to host*

With back-to-school shopping and getting the family ready for the first day of school, this is a busy time of year to be a parent, isn't it? If you know busy parents who've been running around taking care of the needs of everyone else, and you want a fun way to give them a break, let's chat. Whether you host a brunch on the first day of school, or a party that week, time at your house will be something for them to look forward to. *Oh, by the way*, our program includes a number of menu choices, so we would tailor your event to be exactly what you want it to be!

EXAMPLE #6: *You're selling the opportunity to host*

Our hostesses really enjoy the experience of seeing their friends. They're delighted when they see how many free and discounted products they earn for hosting a get-together. *Oh, by the way*, did I mention that our hostesses this month will also earn this popular product? Reaction to this promotion has been amazing, I've got just a few dates left this month. Let's talk about a date that might work for you!

Keep a favorite feature or benefit in your back pocket.

EXAMPLE #7: You're selling a business opportunity

It sounds like you're really excited about our company's business opportunity, and I'm excited with you! ***Oh, by the way***, I forgot to mention that we have a special start-up bonus program going on right now. New Consultants who enroll by the end of this month can earn an extra bonus product. How great would it be to choose one of these three popular products to come with your Starter Kit?

EXAMPLE #8: You're selling a business opportunity

You've asked some great questions today — you're really thinking about this, aren't you? Oh, I almost forgot to tell you. Our new contest period starts the first of next month. You'd be coming in right at the start of the contest period — your timing couldn't be better!

EXAMPLE #9: You're selling a business opportunity

You mentioned that you're looking for income right away. ***Oh, by the way*** — in our company, you don't have to wait for a commission payment — you take your commission at the time of the sale. So the sooner you start doing parties, the sooner you'll have dollars to spend. How would it feel to contribute to the family budget right away?

RECAP

As a sales professional, experience will help you pace your presentation and delivery of product ideas and information. Keep working to keep your customers and prospective team members engaged and with you every step of the way. It gets easier the more you do it.

Just as delivering a good joke means not releasing the punchline too early, your sales presentation will work best when you save one exciting benefit for the end. One well-timed statement can move a customer's thought process from 99% **thinking** to 100% **sold**. That one little percentage point can make a 100% difference in your business success!

Oh, by the way invites you to put a smile on your customer's face. Delight her as you create excitement for your special offer, a compelling feature, or a surprise about the product. Pique your customer's interest in your products — and keep interest high by saving a fun and exciting benefit for the end.

*It's up to me
to make selling fun.*

Oh, by the way ...
WORKS WELL WHEN:

- You know of a product feature that commonly creates a *wow* response. Instead of leading with the *wow*, you can save this feature to add impact at the end.

- You are selling something that partners well with another product. Solidify interest in each item independently before calling attention to how well they work together.

- You're offering the product at a special price savings or you have an add-on offer with time sensitivity. Establish interest in the product at full retail price first, then allow the special offer to create a sense of urgency.

- The product has unexpected functionality beyond what is obvious. Create interest in the product for its stated purpose, then generate *oohs* and *aahs* as you go on to show its versatility.

- You're promoting the benefits of hosting. Build interest in the experience first, and the free products second.

QUESTIONS FOR REFLECTION

- As I think about my favorite products, what are some of the compelling features that would lend themselves to being tucked into my "back pocket?"

- What's the best way for me to learn more about pacing my sales presentations?

- How am I thinking differently about sharing my company's special offers?

- Which host benefits are most likely to lead to a prospective hostess deciding to say "yes" to my invitation to book? How can I modify the pace of my presentation and conversations to shine a brighter light on those benefits?

- What have I found to be the most reassuring words I can offer a person who is thinking about getting involved with the business? How can I shift my recruiting conversations to place those words at the right place in my conversations?

SOMETIMES, WHEN
YOU'RE SELLING . . .

. . . *you help your customer*

find a way

to solve a problem.

Let's look at a story.

CHAPTER | # 12

If we could find a way

Work together to explore solutions.

Like many moms, I volunteered to serve on the PTA Board to get involved with my children's school. At the time, it didn't seem like much of a commitment. The Board met just once a month during the school year. Board members, if they chose to, could get involved in other optional projects throughout the year.

It was September, and it was the second Board meeting of the school year. The meeting was well-attended, and enthusiasm was high. Everyone gathered around the tables, carefully arranged in a U-shaped design in the center of the school library.

At 7:30 p.m., the meeting began with the usual call to order. First we heard committee updates. Then the principal stood up. She said, *We won't have an update on the status of the Spring Carnival tonight. That's because we don't yet have a Committee Chair for that important project. Did you know that the Spring Carnival is our organization's primary source of income? We are counting on that for a number of things this year. So if you would like to head up that important effort, let me know.* She picked up a green clipboard with the signup sheet and a #2 pencil. She handed the clipboard to the first person to her left, and proceeded through her agenda. As the mother of boys, I am accustomed to seeing things fly by at a very rapid pace. What I didn't expect to see was the clipboard flying around the table in less than thirty seconds, passed from person to person like a hot potato.

The next morning after the boys left for school, I received a phone call from the school principal. *Sue,* she said, *I was surprised to see that no one signed up to chair the Spring Carnival. I got to thinking about who I'd like to see in that role, and thought of you. You are my first call this morning because you are organized and you are someone I can count on to get things done. I understand you are busy. You may be thinking this is more work than you have time for. **If we could find a way** that you could take the lead, backed by a good team supporting you to get the work done, would it be something you'd be willing to think about?*

About twelve hours earlier, the same invitation was presented to me on a bright green clipboard and I passed. This time was different. The principal thought not only about the opportunity she was selling, but also about me. She was willing to work with me to come up with a way to make it work.

If you had to guess, what do you think I said?

CONCEPT OVERVIEW

Sometimes a customer dismisses an idea or product before even thinking about how it could benefit her. Customers might need your help to move past initial conclusions about your product. When your customer tells you that something just won't work for her, it's not a stop sign, it's an opportunity to help her think further.

The phrase, *If we could find a way*, helps you accomplish two objectives:

1. It helps you identify whether that single hesitation is the only one getting in the way. In a sense, you find out if everything else about the idea is good — before you start exploring solutions.

2. It's a great opening phrase to show that you want to help your customer find a solution. Notice the difference between saying *if I could tell you a way* and saying ***if we could find a way***. The key difference is *we*.

When you use this soft-selling phrase, you're not telling your customer that you're going to give her more reasons to buy. You're telling her that the two of you, together, are going to explore ways for her to get what she wants and needs.

YOU CAN SAY . . .

- ***If we could find a way . . .***
- Let's put our heads together and find a solution.
- ***If we could find a way*** to work around the concern you've just shared, would you want to keep looking at this?

Let's look at some examples of this concept in action.

EXAMPLES

EXAMPLE #1: *You're selling home décor*

I noticed you looking at the pieces of our special bath kit. I can tell you love it! . . . Oh, you say that you think this wouldn't match the rest of your décor? I see. *If we could find a way* to make this work with the other things you have in the bathroom, would it be something you'd consider?

EXAMPLE #2: Y*ou're selling scrapbooking products*

You mentioned that you have a graduation party coming up. I love your idea of making handmade invitations for the party. I completely understand that ideas like this sometimes seem like they might take a lot of time. *If we could find a way* to make your project a little simpler using our easy software, would this be something you'd want to look at?

EXAMPLE #3: *You're selling jewelry*

Yes, this necklace is a little shorter than some of the others. *If we could find a way* to extend the length for you, would that be something you'd want to look at?

EXAMPLE #4: *You're selling the opportunity to host*

I see, you're thinking that a party would be fun, but you don't think you have enough space at your house. *If we could find a way* to make the most of the space you have — and put together a great party, would this be something you'd want to think about?

EXAMPLE #5: *You're selling the opportunity to host*

You are absolutely right. This time of year is busy for everyone, and it sounds like you have a lot going on right now. If we could find a way to fill your house with your friends without spending a lot of extra time, is a party something you'd want to consider?

EXAMPLE #6: *You're selling the opportunity to host*

You may be looking at our host rewards and thinking *Hmmm . . . those benefits sure look great, but I'm not sure I know enough people to put together a party.* I think you'd be surprised! *If we could find a way* for you to fill your living room, just like our hostess has tonight, would hosting be something you'd like to learn more about?

EXAMPLE #7: *You're selling a business opportunity*

So, you're feeling like it might not work for you to be a Consultant because your husband travels so much — is that right? I understand. I'm wondering, *if we could find a way* for you to earn a great income and have fun doing it — while working around your husband's travel schedule — would getting involved be something you'd want to learn about?

EXAMPLE #8: *You're selling a business opportunity*

. . . You like the idea of earning a good income, but you're not sure you have enough time to make a business work. I understand! *If we could find a way* for you to take the 8-10 hours a week you said you had available, and really make the most of that time, would you want to take a look at this? What if we started by seeing what you could earn working just 8 hours a week?

EXAMPLE #9: *You're selling a business opportunity*

I understand, you feel like you're not creative enough for a business like this. You'd be surprised. A lot of people think that. *If we could find a way* to take what you're seeing as a disadvantage — that you aren't especially creative — and turn it into an advantage for you, would this be something you'd want to explore?

RECAP

Effective sales professionals know that selling is more than telling. Selling is thinking like the customer. It is gently working with her to help her see how your products and services can enhance her life. One of the strengths of the direct selling business model is personalized interaction. While experienced sellers come to recognize common concerns and hesitations, they know that success means meeting each customer where she is.

A customer's hesitations are opportunities in disguise. Each hesitation provides you with an opportunity to help your customer find the encouragement she needs and to find a customized solution. It's tempting (and usually quicker) to try to solve a problem for someone else, thinking that what has worked for one person is likely to work for another. A softer, more effective approach is to invite customers to partner with you to explore possibilities. To work together.

If we could find a way is a valuable tool in helping you become clearer about whether the hesitation you hear is really the one that's in the way. This phrase also serves to remind you to partner with your customer. As you work together to find solutions, your customer will be more likely to feel invested in the outcome.

***Is there really such a thing as
"one size fits all?"***

If we could find a way ...
WORKS WELL WHEN:

- You're selling one-on-one, and you want to get to the heart of the individual's hesitations.

- You can sense that your customer or prospective team member really wants something, but she's getting in her own way.

- You are working with a long-term recruiting prospect with a pattern of indecisiveness.

- Interactions with your customer or recruiting prospect have given you the impression that fear is holding her back.

- You have ideas, and you know that it won't work to toss them out at your customer. You want to partner with your customer to explore solutions.

QUESTIONS FOR REFLECTION

- Can I think of a time when someone took the time to help me think through a solution? What was the impact of that conversation?

- In the past, what has made me feel inclined to solve problems for my customers, hostesses, or recruit prospects? What benefits do I see to discovering solutions together?

- When I'm talking with people about my business, what concerns do they immediately raise? What alternatives do I have to one-size-fits-all comebacks?

- How do I feel when I help a customer, hostess, or prospective recruit break through a concern?

- At what point in the recruiting process would I be most likely to use the phrase *if we could find a way?*

SOMETIMES, WHEN YOU'RE SELLING . . .

. . . someone wants to feel like you

are talking just to her.

If you are someone who

makes an immediate connection.

Let's look at a story.

CHAPTER | 13

If you are someone who

No one wants to be anyone.
Everyone wants to be someone.

Some days I wondered if what I was doing as a direct seller made much of a difference in the world.

When I'd see a news story about a heroic firefighter, I'd question the significance of selling cookware at home parties. One such day of self-doubt, I sang in the choir at the funeral of one of my fellow choir members. Rita and I hadn't known each other well, but I knew she was a loving wife, mother, and a great alto. She wasn't given much time after her breast cancer diagnosis to say good-bye to the people she treasured.

At her funeral, I listened as friends and family spoke about what her life meant to them. I pondered, *Life can be so short. Am I really living my life to its fullest?*

After the funeral, I went home to get myself ready for a home show that evening. Gathering catalogs, order forms, and show materials, I felt like I was going through the motions. I thought, *What in the world am I doing? I can't do this show tonight. How am I going to stand up there and act like I'm excited about a bunch of products?* Somehow I talked myself into going. It helped to recall my last conversation with the hostess, how excited she was about the number of people coming to her house. That matters, I thought.

After a quick family dinner, it was time to leave for my show. Before stepping out the door, I kissed each of the guys on the forehead, wishing them a nice evening with Dad. *Have a good show, Mom,* they said as I walked out the back door. *That matters,* I thought.

With a lot of time to think during my drive, I started with a little pity party over having to work instead of being home with my family. And then I got to thinking about my hostess, and how tonight's get-together was important to her. I thought about a customer who had recently told me how one of our cookbooks inspired her to have an afternoon of baking with her daughter. My thoughts turned to my sons, and how they were spending bonding time with Dad tonight. *That stuff matters,* I thought.

A lot of people showed up that night, and my hostess was thrilled. After guests introduced themselves, I spontaneously said this: ***If you are someone who*** *ever wonders if the little things you do each day make a difference, know this. Tonight I'll be sharing products that on the surface, look like cooking tools. But they can create some pretty amazing moments. As you share time with each other tonight, know that you being here means a great deal to Robin, and it does to me, too.* ***If you are someone who*** *has ever wondered what it's like to be in a business like this, know that it's people like you who make it feel worthwhile.*

If you have ever wondered how to really connect, know that nothing works as effectively as you being you. That night, I left with more recruiting leads than ever before.

CONCEPT OVERVIEW

Every so often, we feel like someone is talking just to us. Usually, that's when the person is speaking from the heart. You know that the product or service you're about to sell could be a match for people of all shapes or sizes, all ages or stages of life. This is a product which could make a difference in anyone's life. Yet, you're not likely to make an emotional connection by saying *this can be for anyone*. No one wants to be anyone. Everyone wants to be someone.

If you are someone who helps you position your product or service in a way so people identify with it on an emotional level. You use these words to call out experiences which people may appreciate. You're not calling out life circumstances which suggest this is an ideal product; you're calling out characteristics which might describe a person as she is enjoying your product.

In a sense, you want your customer to hear what you say and feel a real connection. You want her inner voice to say, *Yes, that is ME!*

YOU CAN SAY . . .

- *If you are someone who* enjoys . . .

- *If you are someone who* is known for . . .

- *If you are someone who* would like more . . .

Let's look at some examples of this concept in action.

EXAMPLES

EXAMPLE #1: *You're selling kitchen tools*
If you are someone (like a lot of us!) who enjoys cooking, but you don't enjoy all of the cleanup that comes afterwards, this is for you. Take a look at this . . .

EXAMPLE #2: *You're selling cosmetics and skin care*
Up to now you may have gotten by without a skin care routine — and you are wondering if any of these products will amount to any measurable difference. Or, you may be someone who is used to a routine, but maybe not completely used to the way that time has changed your skin's look and feel. No matter what, *if you are someone who* would like to love the face you see in the mirror every morning, our skin care collection is right for you. Let's look at how to find the program that fits your life and your skin type.

EXAMPLE #3: *You're selling gift items*
If you are someone who is known for being thoughtful, you're going to love what I'm about to show you. This will show how much you care. And, it's so distinctive that you're going to stand out from the crowd. Let's take a look.

EXAMPLE #4: *You're selling the opportunity to host*

If you are someone who has ever run into a friend at the grocery store, and said *let's get together some time* . . . and then, you felt a little guilty because life got in the way . . . you may really enjoy the experience of having a party. Isn't catching up with friends like you're doing tonight much more fun than trying to catch up in Aisle Six, next to the peanut butter?

EXAMPLE #5: *You're selling the opportunity to host*

Do you like to entertain? Do you like it even more when it's easy? *If you're someone who* has so much fun when you throw a party, you tell yourself that you should do it more often ... let's talk about doing the next party at your house. Mary, will you take just a minute to tell us about your experience? What was it like for you to put this party together?

EXAMPLE #6: *You're selling the opportunity to host*

Have you seen a thing or two tonight which has captured your interest? *If you're someone who* has a few more things on your wish list than your budget allows, you might want to think about having a party. Here's what our hostesses love most about our reward program . . .

EXAMPLE #7: *You're selling a business opportunity*

If you are someone who really enjoys being around people, let's talk for a minute about how this business could be a good fit for you. What people love most is the way it makes them feel about themselves — and how great it is that work means socializing with people like you!

EXAMPLE #8: *You're selling a business opportunity*
Have you ever wondered what it would be like to be in business for yourself? *If you are someone who* likes the idea of being your own boss, I invite you to think about doing what I'm doing. What people discover is a great feeling of independence when they realize that they're really in charge of their life.

EXAMPLE #9: *You're selling a business opportunity*
Are you someone who likes being around people? *If you're someone who* likes to have fun — and likes to help other people have fun — I'd love to tell you more about becoming a Consultant with our company. It's a business for people who like being around other people.

RECAP

Most direct sellers represent a diverse product line with appeal that's broad enough to allow most anyone to find something they would enjoy. And many of the products you sell have universal appeal. Yet in sending a message that your products could be right for anyone, you may miss out on the opportunity to connect with a person's emotional needs and individuality.

If you are someone who invites you to connect with something inside each one of your customers, helping them identify something about themselves that makes them right for the product you're talking about. This phrase encourages you to speak more from your heart than from your head, connecting with what matters.

If you are someone who is not your way to call out specific life circumstances with hopes that the one person in that exact situation will recognize herself. *If you are someone who* invites you to reach out to many people, calling out characteristics to identify themselves as "just right" for what you're telling them about.

***Today, someone needs
what I have to offer.***

If you are someone who . . . WORKS WELL WHEN:

- You have a sense that customers think that products like yours are for someone else, not them.

- You are selling a product with universal appeal, yet you want your customer to feel like it was made for her.

- The product you are selling can be directly connected to a common emotional want or need.

- You're selling something intangible, such as a service or a business opportunity.

When you are selling without the benefit of a visual aid or sample, it helps to remember one of the distinctions between a demonstrator and a sales professional. **Product demonstrators** focus on a product, and **sales professionals** focus on people. *If you are someone who* leads you to connect in a manner that has your customer feeling like you are speaking exclusively to her.

QUESTIONS FOR REFLECTION

- If I was to describe the ideal customer, a person who would be most likely to love the products I sell, what words would I choose?

- Now — what can I say in my selling conversations to make connections with people like this?

- What can I do to make more of my customers feel like my products were made just for them?

- What do my most satisfied hostesses have in common? (Consider their characteristics, not their life circumstances.)

- What can I say to connect with more hostesses like this?

SOMETIMES, WHEN
YOU'RE SELLING . . .

. . . *your customer just needs*

a little bit of validation

that she has made a

great choice.

Let's look at a story.

CHAPTER | 14

Great Choice

Validate your customer's feelings about choices.

I discovered in my selling career that challenges have a way of putting pep in my step. For me, that's just the way it is.

It had been a dozen years since I started my business. My team was thriving and I had plenty to do to keep the business moving forward. Yet, my work didn't feel new anymore. Often, I showed up feeling uninspired and complacent. My inner voice shouted, *Sue — it is time to commit yourself to a NEW challenge.* My instinct told me it was time to find a challenge which did not involve my business.

For years, I'd wanted to do what I had seen countless others do — fill otherwise ordinary moments with the delicious sound of music. On February 19, 1996, what would have been my mom's 76th birthday, I made the decision that it was time to buy myself a piano. Not just any piano. A beautiful piano. A white piano. I first saw it on the showroom floor at a music store. I wrote a check.

The next day, the delivery truck arrived and I watched expectantly as the door rolled open. Immediately, I felt the inner struggle that sometimes sets in after making an emotional purchase. One moment I would tell myself, *This is SO exciting!* Seconds later, I would say, *What in the WORLD have I done?* Seriously. I tried to recall the way I felt when I first saw the piano on the showroom floor. As this huge instrument tried to find its way into my mind and my living room, I started second-guessing my decision. Maybe I should have started with a small electronic keyboard, and upgraded to a real piano once I learned how to play.

David, the delivery supervisor, announced that the setup was complete. He invited me to sit down and play for a few minutes to be sure everything was OK. My only option was to admit that I didn't know how to play. David offered a reassuring smile as he asked, *Would it be ok if I played for awhile?* I don't know how David knew that I would absolutely love the sound of Bruce Hornsby's *"The Way It Is"*, but that's what he selected to introduce my new piano to my heart and my home. As his fingers danced skillfully across the black and white keys, he looked up and said, *This is a beautiful piano, isn't it?* ***Great choice!***

He demonstrated how opening the top of the piano created an even richer sound. As he kept playing, I could feel the music bouncing off my hardwood floors. The joyful sound of a fresh, new challenge resonated in my heart. I was inspired. I reminded myself that my decision to buy this piano was, indeed, a ***great choice***.

CONCEPT OVERVIEW

Do you appreciate a little reassurance after you've made a purchase? I do, too. You may have thought that after your customer makes a purchasing decision, your work was done. Experienced sellers know that it is just beginning. At times, logic has a louder voice than emotion. Customers can quickly move from making a buying decision to finding ways to talk themselves right out of the buying decision they've just made.

This one's easy. It falls after a buying decision has been made, when your goal is to help your customer feel good about a **great choice**. Whether you're making a reassuring phone call the morning after a customer places an order, or you step into a validating conversation at the point of the sale, you want to find ways to remind her of the soft, emotional benefits of her recent purchase. Validate the decision to schedule a date.

If you have a minute or two to chat at the order table, invite your customer to tell you how she envisions the product in her life. Share a few ideas to enhance the way she thinks. Send her home feeling confident in her decisions. Validate her feelings . . . and her **great choice!**

YOU CAN SAY . . .

- **Great choice!** Did you choose this as a gift, or is this for you?

- **Great choice**, this is one of my favorites, too. I use it this way . . .

- **Great choice!** I just heard a great idea. Did you know . . .

Let's look at some examples of this concept in action.

EXAMPLES

EXAMPLE#1: *You're selling home decor*
You're going to love this platter. ***Great choice!*** Were you talking with our hostess about this? This product is one of her favorites, too. Check out how great this platter looks on her table with cheese and crackers.

EXAMPLE #2: *You're selling jewelry*
This necklace is going to look great on you — I loved when you tried it on with the sweater you're wearing tonight. ***Great choice!***

EXAMPLE #3: *You're selling scrapbooking products*
Great choice! You're going to love this collection of bridal products. I'm guessing you have a special event coming up. Is this something you chose as a gift for yourself, or are you planning to create a gift for someone else?

EXAMPLE #4: *You're selling the opportunity to host*
Are you thinking about what it would be like to get together with your friends and family at a party like this? When Leslie and I were talking earlier, she told me how much she was looking forward to seeing all of you tonight. Leslie, would you agree you made a ***great choice*** to host this get-together tonight? How does it feel to see friends you haven't seen for awhile?

EXAMPLE #5: *You're selling the opportunity to host*

What do you enjoy most about having friends over to your house? Do you love when they stop to look at the pictures you took so much time to put up on the wall? Or when they comment on your amazing chocolate raspberry brownies? Do you love it when friends who haven't met each other get to know each other? When I think back to the hostesses I've been fortunate to work with, I've heard all of those things — and more. I especially love it when a hostess tells me that hosting a party was a ***great choice***. How she's thankful that she decided to jump in and get her friends together. What about you? What would make hosting a great choice in your life right now?

EXAMPLE #6: *You're validating the decision to host*

I know how busy you are, and it was hard to find a date that would work for you. You made a ***great choice*** to host in May. What people love about getting together at that time of year is . . .

EXAMPLE #7: *You're selling a business opportunity*

A lot of people wait for the perfect time to start something new. Sometimes people wait so long for the perfect time that they never begin. I know you have a lot going on right now, Debbie. I'm wondering what would make getting involved a ***great choice*** in your life right now?

EXAMPLE #8: *You're validating a decision to start the business*

Karen, I know it was hard for you to decide between our Starter Kit options. I think you've made a ***great choice*** here. What you're going to love about the kit you selected is . . .

EXAMPLE #9: You're validating the decision to start a business

I'm really looking forward to working with you. I hope you're as excited as I am to see your business get off the ground. I know you've been thinking about this since you had your party a few months ago, and from what I can tell, it wasn't an easy decision for you. You made a ***great choice*** — to invest in your future. Really, what you've done is invest in yourself! I can see you doing really well with this business.

RECAP

Give your customer plenty of reasons to feel good about her decision to purchase a product, schedule a get-together, or explore your company's business opportunity. Sometimes a step as simple as sharing another product tip will help her feel more solid about her decision.

When time permits, you can invite your customer to share an idea with you. You can chat about how she plans to use the product she's ordering, or ask what she's most looking forward to about having the new item. As she shares her positive thoughts out loud, she will cement them in her own mind, reducing the likelihood that she'll talk herself out of her buying decision.

Leave your customer feeling inspired to wake up the next day hearing a voice inside. Not the voice of doubt. The voice that reminds her that she has made a ***great choice***.

It's up to me
to move from selling to serving.

Great choice
WORKS WELL WHEN:

- Your customer places a significant order.

- You have an idea to share. There isn't enough time during your sales presentation to share all the features of the product your customer has chosen.

- Your customer has purchased one of your personal favorites.

- Your customer took a long time to make a decision.

- You notice that your customer ordered an item you didn't even mention during the presentation, and you want her to feel great about her choice.

- Your upcoming hostess seems nervous about her decision to schedule a party.

QUESTIONS FOR REFLECTION

- Have I ever second-guessed a personal buying decision? What did it take for me to feel good about making that purchase?

- What choices are difficult for my customers to make?

- How can taking steps to reinforce my customers' choices make a difference in my business?

- What keeps me from taking the time to thank my customers, reminding them that they made a *great choice* to order a product?

- In what ways do I believe that my own decision to get involved in direct sales was a *great choice?*

GETTING STARTED
WITH SAYING IT SOFTLY

- **Get started one phrase at a time.** Some phrases will feel more natural than others. Make subtle shifts in your selling vocabulary by incorporating just one chapter at a time. Weave one *story-starter* into your style until it becomes comfortable.

- **Practice at home.** You can accelerate your learning by practicing with something other than your own products. Choose a common household item, such as a bar of soap, a tennis shoe, or a package of fabric softening sheets. Practice *saying it softly* phrases as if you are selling the item. You'll learn the selling concepts quickly because you won't be distracted by the features of your own products.

- **Practice with co-workers.** Get together with team members to practice selling. Take turns assuming the role of customer and sales professional. Share helpful feedback with each other as you fine-tune your skills.

- **Make it your own.** Selling is most effective when you show up to the sales presentation as yourself. If a word or phrase doesn't feel comfortable, don't force it. You may hear yourself using *story starters* in everyday conversation. It's possible that your family members will not notice at all. Possible. Or, they may giggle when they hear you *saying it softly* in all that you do.

CONCLUSION

CONCLUSION

A soft style of doing business. It's warm. It's welcoming. It's a business that produces significant, measurable results — and a business that lets you be yourself. ***Selling it softly*** isn't pushing — it's making what you have to sell so compelling that people feel drawn to you, your company, and your products.

Invite that part of you that wants to do more than just sell a product — that wants to serve, to make a difference in the lives of others — to come out and play.

Are you thinking differently about yourself and your business? As a fellow entrepreneur, I've noticed that it's rarely what we *know*, it's what we *do*, that makes the biggest difference. One secret to getting ahead is getting started. I know I'm not the first person to suggest that it's up to you to make your business what you want it to be. Who will you call to schedule more business? When will you get started?

Until now, you may have spent a lot of time thinking of creative ways to say . . . *I am not a salesperson*. What if, instead of hiding the fact that you're in sales, you felt so good about selling that you started to stand taller? *Head held high. Shoulders back. Look out world, here I am* kind of tall. Selling is your way of serving, and it's something to be proud of.

You may, until now, have looked for creative ways to say *I am not a recruiter*. After all, *recruiter* is not the softest of words. As you're stretching and growing, it is natural for you to want to share the experience of your business with others. How will it feel to help others get what they really want — more confidence, more satisfying relationships, and more success?

Whether you started selling as a way to fill a few gaps in your budget or to build a long-term career, you have in your hands a business with endless possibilities. Each step you take with your business of selling is an opportunity for you to serve. Observe the people around you. Pay attention to what they say about themselves and their lives. Focus on how you can help. Confidently bring your soft-selling style to the work that you do.

What makes the idea of creating your own story of success really matter to *you?* Without a clearly defined purpose, it all feels like hard work. Successful entrepreneurs know this: *When we know what makes the business matter, we find a way to do what needs to be done.*

When you know why you're doing something, you're willing to work harder than you thought possible. But here's the thing. It doesn't have to feel like hard work.

How will your story of success unfold?

Imagine a living room with a group of guests gathered for your party presentation. Picture yourself catching a glimpse of a guest as she takes her first sip of wine. As you see her settle into the softness of an overstuffed chair, you can almost hear her say, *Aahhhh.* You feel good knowing that what she's about to experience can make a difference in her life. It's clear that she needs a break from her life challenges. You stand tall as you step up to start the party. You're confident in yourself and in the power of your company's mission. You've carefully thought about products you're about to share.

> *You may be thinking* . . . *I'm not confident yet. I like what I'm learning, but I'm not sure how to put all of this into practice.*

Your toughest choice will be to decide which ways of saying it softly you will add to your party presentation first.

What people tell me works best is to start with one phrase —any of the ten we explored — until you feel as comfortable with those words as that guest feels settling into an overstuffed chair. As you've been reading, has your mind been thinking of the many places you can experiment with your new soft-selling style?

Have you thought about the ways this new approach will make a difference in your business? In your life? Believe it. When you get better at selling, you will do whatever you set your mind to.

If we could find a way for you to embrace your role as a salesperson, knowing that selling is your way of serving, would the journey be worthwhile? Imagine the possibilities.

If you are someone who gets excited about new challenges, your future looks bright! Once you learn to sell, there's nothing you can't do.

So, what that means to you is that every element of your success will build upon your refreshed confidence, skills, and passion for the business of selling. You may encounter obstacles on your path to success. Don't let yourself be one of them. Manage yourself. Help people feel better, not just about making dinner, looking prettier, or finding the just-right color to decorate, but by helping them feel better about their lives. Help them feel better about *themselves*.

You have made a ***great choice*** to get involved in your business, and to increase your sales, parties, and recruiting results. Each day, remind yourself that others need — and want — what you have to share. It's up to you to inspire them, and to show how your products and services can make a difference in their lives.

Oh, by the way . . . it will be fun to discover how your new soft-selling approach touches other dimensions of your life. You may even hear yourself ***saying it softly*** the next time you invite your four-year-old to pick up her toys. Oh, and I forgot to mention, ***selling it softly*** increases your earnings, too!

Selling is the art of influence. I wish you the best as you create your own story of direct selling success.

ACKNOWLEDGEMENTS

In a book that's about creating stories, I am delighted to honor and appreciate the many people who played a role in creating the story of *Selling it Softly*.

I open with a heartfelt thank you to my husband, Matt. I am grateful for your constant belief in me and your unending support of my entrepreneurial adventures. You've always been my most trusted advisor and biggest supporter. With love and affection, I thank you.

To each of my three sons, thank you. I deeply appreciate you for giving me reasons to feel purposeful, inspired, and truly proud. Clint, I especially appreciate you for standing tall in your service to others, and for your kind acknowledgement that my chosen work has been worthwhile. Jeff, thank you for the fun during the time you spent working with me, and thank you for inspiring me with the way you embrace new adventures and new goals. Doug, thank you for each conversation about the art of business and consulting, and I especially appreciate the way you've applied your emotional intelligence to create success.

Thank you to the friends and family members who have encouraged me every step of the way. You know who you are, and I'm thankful for you.

Thank you to my editor, Susan Iida-Pederson. You helped me find my voice and nurtured my journey to become an author. I appreciate the exceptional level of respect you showed to me, to every word, and to every reader.

To Tom Guetzke, thank you for sharing the experience of writing our books. I have appreciated keeping each other accountable and sharing joy as we've inched toward the finish line.

To Laurie Girardi, thank you for embracing my soft-selling concepts and keeping them alive with such enthusiasm.

Thank you to Celie O'Meara, Cindy Brueck, and Joni McPherson for your excellent work with graphic design. Thank you to Daniel Kieffer and Lee Harrelson for sharing your expertise in creating beautiful photographs.

Thank you to Shelly Chrisman for gently coercing my computer to cooperate, no matter what hour of the day. I appreciate your constant support.

To Gordon Stagg, thank you for introducing me to the art and joy of consulting.

To Bonni Davis, thank you for taking time out of your busy schedule to read my manuscript, offer insightful feedback, and share a quote.

To Cindy Monroe, thank you writing words for the book's cover that inspire readers to open the pages, urging them to learn and grow.

To Jill Blashack Strahan, I appreciate your reminder that writing is a way to help others change their lives. And I thank you for writing words to enhance my book's cover.

I appreciate the many people who have taken the time to share valuable insights along the way. To Mark LeBlanc, thank you for encouraging me to stay proud every step of the way. To Audrey Thomas, I appreciate your advice to find the stamina to just get it done. To David Levin, I appreciate your encouraging words, and your generous spirit in sharing contacts made and lessons learned.

To the many customers and hostesses who opened your homes and your hearts, thank you. Without you, I would not have discovered the joy of selling.

Thank you to Doris Christopher for creating a company that

provides opportunities for people to discover and cultivate their entrepreneurial spirit. I am deeply grateful to Pampered Chef® colleagues, staff members, and team members who made the journey interesting, a lot of fun, and an amazing learning experience.

Thank you to everyone who was part of Big Yellow Box by Crayola® — both at the company and in the field — for your dedication as we created, connected, and discovered.

To the many clients I've been privileged to work with and still work with today, thank you. You have opened new doors and created opportunities to learn and grow together.

And to you, the reader, thank you. I appreciate that you've decided to explore a new way of thinking about yourself, your business, and the art of *Selling it Softly*.

Sue Rusch works with sales organizations as a speaker, consultant and strategic advisor to top executives and sales leaders. Sue is a Certified Speaking Professional (CSP), the speaking industry's international measure of speaking experience and skill.

To contact Sue Rusch or to inquire about booking her to speak for your organization, visit:

www.SueRusch.com

Or, contact her at:

Sue Rusch
c/o Grand Oaks Press
7455 France Avenue South #507
Minneapolis, MN   55435

To inquire about quantity order discounts:
www.suerusch.com/contacts

ABOUT THE AUTHOR

 Sue Rusch is known for building a nationally-recognized $19 Million field sales organization, and for inspiring thousands to think differently about themselves and their businesses. Her sharp insights are drawn from a depth of experience on both the field and corporate sides of the direct selling industry. From an award-winning field leader with The Pampered Chef® to Vice President and General Manager of Big Yellow Box by Crayola® (a Hallmark Company), Sue developed a passion for entrepreneurial success. Today, she serves as a speaker, consultant, and strategic advisor to top sales executives and sales leaders.

Sue and her husband reside in Minneapolis, Minnesota, where they raised their three grown sons.